woman&home Christmas Cookbook
© 2024 Future Publishing Limited

Future Books is an imprint of Future PLC
Quay House, The Ambury, Bath, BA1 1UA

A catalogue record for this book is
available from the British Library.

ISBN 978-1-80521-764-0 hardback

The paper holds full FSC certification
and accreditation.

Printed in Turkey by Ömür Printing, for Future PLC

Interested in Foreign Rights to publish this title?
Email us at:
licensing@futurenet.com

Group Editor
Philippa Grafton

Art Editor
Madelene King

Group Food Director
Jen Bedloe

Group Editor, woman&home
Hannah Fernando

Senior Art Editor
Andy Downes

Head of Art & Design
Greg Whitaker

Editorial Director
Jon White

Managing Director
Grainne McKenna

Production Project Manager
Matthew Eglinton

Global Business Development Manager
Jennifer Smith

Senior International Trade Marketing Associate
Kate Waldock

Head of Future International & Bookazines
Tim Mathers

Cover images
Chris Alack / futurecontenthub.com

Future plc is a public company
quoted on the London Stock
Exchange
(symbol: FUTR)
www.futureplc.com

Chief Executive Officer **Jon Steinberg**
Non-Executive Chairman **Richard Huntingford**
Chief Financial and Strategy Officer **Penny Ladkin-Brand**

Tel +44 (0)1225 442 244

woman&home
CHRISTMAS
Cookbook

Welcome to the
woman&home
CHRISTMAS
Cookbook

Treasured moments with family and friends, time off work to wind down and relax, snuggles under a blanket with a festive film on the TV – there's a lot to love about the winter holidays, but undoubtedly one of the best things about Christmas is the abundance of food and drink! When you're the host, however, the magic quickly wears off as you stress over oven timings, runny gravy and keeping everyone entertained while you toil away.

Over the following pages, we've pulled together some of our favourite simple and satisfying winter recipes, from delicious nibbles and aperitifs to please your guests, to traditional roasts and sides for the family feast. We've also shared some of our most popular seasonal bakes, including divine yule logs and Christmas puddings that don't require weeks of preparation.

Elsewhere we've got you covered for ideas for floral centrepieces, and our experts reveal the party planning, home décor and stress-busting tips you need to make hosting a breeze.

W&H *Contents*

30 Smoked salmon canapés

10
Party planning
tricks to make
Christmas a
breeze!

56 Brie and sweet onion tarts

74 Herb-rolled leg of lamb

124 Nougat cheesecake

It's time to GET FESTIVE

From decorating your tree to cooking up those festive favourites, there's so much to think about at Christmas. Here, we bring you the best party planning, home décor and mindfulness tips – guaranteed to keep you calm and help you be the hostess with the mostest!

WORDS BY *Sophie Barton*

It's the most joyful time of year, but Christmas can leave us feeling a little overwhelmed at times. So, what's the secret to making everything run smoothly, without the stress? According to our experts, a bit of clever planning and preparation is all it takes.

You'll find the next few pages packed with their simple, practical tips, ranging from easy yet effective décor ideas to effortless ways to add elegance with flowers. Our fool-proof Christmas countdown guide will make light work of entertaining, too – our party pros take you step by step through the build-up to the big day, showing you how you can make it fun and fuss-free.

And for those moments when you do feel a little frazzled or fatigued, our psychologists give their top tricks for busting stress and boosting your mood. From five-minute fixes to easy mindfulness exercises, their tips will help you swap the pressure of hosting Christmas for inner peace. Turn the page to find out more...

Your Christmas COUNTDOWN!

Hosting on Christmas Day may seem like a daunting task, but our stress-busting step-by-step guide will see you through

ONE MONTH BEFORE

"Your first step is to plan those core Christmas meals, then write your shopping list," says Alexandra Dudley, who runs 'How to host a dinner party' events at Soho House. "Include essentials like bin bags, foil, freezer bags and dishwasher tablets."

Now is the time to order your turkey, cheeses, fresh flowers and alcohol. Free up valuable freezer and fridge space by clearing out anything unwanted, and declutter worksurfaces, too.

"Make your Christmas cake, if you haven't already," says Alexandra. "And think about gravy. Save hassle by doubling up your gravy quantities whenever you have a roast in December. Freeze it in containers, so you can combine all the delicious flavours on Christmas Day."

THREE WEEKS BEFORE

Add some Christmas magic by decorating your tree and interior. "Hang a festive wreath on your front door," says party professional Liz Taylor, founder of the Taylor Lynn Corporation (www.tlc-ltd.co.uk). "It makes a fabulous feature and screams 'welcome'. Indoors, fill clear glass bowls with battery-operated pea lights and baubles, then arrange them in clusters. Use festive scented candles too." You'll find more great décor ideas overleaf.

Start wrapping presents and get ahead by batch cooking festive favourites. "Cheese straws, mince pies and sausage rolls all freeze well," says Alexandra. "Make and freeze your cranberry sauce and braised red cabbage for Christmas Day, and ice your cake."

©Getty

TWO WEEKS BEFORE

Save a last-minute panic by planning your Christmas glassware and tableware. "Work out what dishes you'll need, and ensure you have enough serving spoons, cutlery, crackers and napkins," says Alexandra, who hosts the podcast *Come to Supper*. "Drill into the detail – will you need one dish for the roast potatoes, or two? Decide on your table plan, check you have enough chairs and write placenames."

Check your glassware, too. "If you're catering for a crowd, consider hiring glasses to save stress," says Liz. "Freeze slices of lemon and lime, so they're ready to pop into glasses."

23RD AND 24TH

Shop for your final fresh produce and collect your turkey, cheese and fresh flowers. "Arranging flowers on 23 December gives them time to come into bud by Christmas Day," says Alexandra (**www.alexandra dudley.com**). "Keep them in a cool place and add any foliage to your table. Chill your white wine, Champagne and soft drinks."

On the 24th, take your gravy, cabbage and cranberry sauce out of the freezer, then prep your turkey. "Get it completely ready in its baking tray, covering it with foil in the fridge so it's ready to go," says Alexandra. "Peel and prep sprouts, parsnips, potatoes and carrots, leaving them in pans of cold salted water overnight. Parboiling potatoes and parsnips means they're ready to pop into the oven on Christmas Day."

Finally, get rid of the peelings and empty every bin. Double line them with two fresh bags, so you have the next one on stand-by. It's not a glamorous task, but you'll thank us for it on Christmas Day.

ONE WEEK BEFORE

Lay the table up to a week beforehand. "It creates a beautiful centrepiece and builds up anticipation," explains Alexandra. "Give dusty glasses, crockery and serving dishes a clean. Iron linen napkins and arrange any candles, lights and decorations – just leave fresh flowers and foliage for now. Put sticky notes into your serving dishes, too, so helpers know where to put the potatoes, sprouts and other veg. It'll save you telling everyone on the day!"

Take time to create a Christmas playlist. "It's worth spending time on this," says Liz, whose clients include Gary Barlow. "Think about how you want the day to ebb and flow, incorporating different music 'zones' for when you're eating, opening presents or sharing drinks." Write out your cooking timetable, too, working backwards from when you want to eat, and stick it somewhere visible.

Deck the HALLS!

From nature-inspired décor to elegant pastels and a playful, nostalgic vibe, here are some of our favourite ways to embrace the Christmas spirit at home this year

©Oliver Perrott / Lights4fun.co.uk

GORGEOUS GARLANDS

For an easy way to add maximum nature-inspired impact, entwine ivies, firs and other evergreens around your bannisters. Dot luscious red berries or even mistletoe among the foliage, then add a hint of sparkle by threading battery-powered LED lights throughout. Strategically placed candles up the ante – opt for safer battery-powered models, like these flameless candles.

DUSKY PINK DELIGHT

Ring the changes and freshen up your Christmas with a sparkling scheme of blush pinks and pastels. Combine soothing dusky hues and a touch of gold or silver twinkle for a sophisticated look. To keep it elegant yet understated, stick to a consistent colour palette across both your tree and tablescape, coordinating crackers, napkins and tablecloth.

NATURAL NOËL

From rolling fields to glassy lakes and leafy forests, the pandemic has seen us seek solace in the great outdoors. Let that connection with the natural world inspire you this Christmas, with an abundance of foliage, nature-themed decorations and natural materials, such as stylish wooden or woven accessories. This look is all about calming colours – think greens, creams and earthy shades, brought to life with gentle touches of gold. When it comes to your dining table, consider adding pine cones, walnuts or even festive fruit into the mix.

WHIMSICAL WONDERS

Why make Christmas a muted affair? Go all out and celebrate in style, with an abundance of cute and kitsch décor ideas, ranging from the whimsical to the downright nostalgic. Think anything and everything that brings back happy childhood memories, from pretty ribbons to rainbows and flamboyant fairy lights. And while you're at it, why not add in some tinsel, too?

CUTE AS CANDY

For extra wow factor, hang your baubles using statement ribbon. Sweet-inspired decorations, like these candy charmers, are sure to appeal to everyone from children to the young at heart.

SHIMMER AND SPARKLE

To inject a spot of fairy-tale magic, introduce a multiplicity of textures – it'll stop the pinks from becoming sickly, too. You'll find the high street awash with blush-coloured baubles, in everything from frosted glass to glitter and even fabulously feathered options.

SCANDINAVIAN STYLE

Set a peaceful, Scandi-inspired scene with soft shades of cream and beige, a ton of texture and the gentle glow of flickering flames. This is a warm, cosy ambience, so think simple, neutral tree decorations, blonde timbers, hessian stockings and candles in lanterns or hurricane lamps. Add hygge by arranging foliage – try eucalyptus and pussy willow – in vases, on mantlepieces and on shelves, and cluster pine cones together in bowls. Thread micro-LED lights amongst them for a twinkling Scandinavian vibe. For a more traditional Nordic feel, add subtle splashes of red, but don't overdo it!

©Cox & Cox

MAKE IT COSY

Max out the cosy factor by draping faux furs, sheepskins and chunky knitted blankets across benches and sofas. Hang paper ornaments, too, or introduce a hand-crafted vibe by weaving greenery through large circular wreaths. Keep your tablescape minimal, with simple pillar candles and creamy tones, interspersed with splashes of green.

Say it with FLOWERS

Flowers and foliage transform your décor in an instant.
Florist Philippa Craddock and the team at McQueen's
Flowers give us their favourite festive blooms

AMARYLLIS

Widely available in vibrant crimson or snowy white, these statuesque, trumpet-shaped flowers certainly pack a festive punch. Cluster a bunch of stems in a tall glass vase, or use potted amaryllis to add drama to your Christmas tablescape.

HELLEBORES

With their bowing heads and earthy tones – from green through to deep reds and snowy pure whites – delicate hellebore stems add elegance to home arrangements. Arrange on their own, place on the edge of larger arrangements, or within petite bud vases.

PAPERWHITE NARCISSUS

These snowy white beauties may look delicate, but their beautiful scent will infiltrate your home. Place a series of small potted forced narcissus bulbs ("forced bulbs" simply allows you to enjoy these spring flowers earlier) into a larger vessel, cover the soil with moss and add upright branches to offer support.

HYACINTHS

Potted hyacinths add a vibrant splash of colour, rich texture and an incredible scent. To max out their impact, fill a basket or terracotta pot and top the soil with a carpet of lush green moss. Position them on the Christmas dining table, where they'll look fabulous with your festive scheme.

RANUNCULUS

With tones ranging from delicate whites and pinks through to moody crimsons and almost black, ranunculus add beautiful drama to arrangements, particularly as their multi-layered petals fully open. They are at their most perfect when simply placed en mass in a clear glass vase.

CLASSIC EVERGREENS

For scent and texture, it's hard to beat these Christmas classics. Sprigs of aromatic eucalyptus look gorgeous in a vase, or gather an armful for a fantastic table runner. With its dark, glossy leaves and vibrant berries, holly makes the perfect accompaniment.

With thanks to *www.philippacraddock.com* and *www.mcqueens.co.uk.*

Slow down & STAY SANE!

The pressure for perfection means the festive season can leave us feeling a little frayed around the edges, but with a few simple tricks you can adjust your mindset and really make the most of this time with your loved ones. Read on for our expert advice on swapping chaos for inner calm this Christmas

CHOOSE *YOUR* PERFECT

"One of the biggest psychological pressures of Christmas is that it comes once a year – and somehow, that means it needs to be 'perfect'," says psychologist Audrey Tang. "But forget the idyllic snapshots on social media or what friends are doing and ask yourself what really makes a happy Christmas for you?" Mindset coach Amy Crumpton agrees: "It is easy to compare ourselves, but it's okay if you bought the Christmas cake instead of making it, it's okay if your wrapping doesn't meet Instagram standards, and it's okay if your children spend the day in their pyjamas. Enjoy Christmas the way you want to."

GET POSITIVE

We are hardwired to look at the negative over the positive, but a daily gratitude practice shifts you into an optimistic mindset, meaning you are less likely to get swept up in the stresses and niggles of the festive season. "Start each day by telling yourself, or writing down, five things you are grateful for," says Amy. "Perhaps you are grateful to be able to see your family, or that your children are happy and healthy. Doing this quick exercise every morning will train your mind to look for the positives, and helps you maintain perspective when little family irritations or other stresses arise."

PACE YOURSELF

Between work dos, friends & family commitments, festive diaries fill up fast. But pacing yourself before Christmas will ensure you haven't crashed by the time the big day rolls around. "Festive fatigue is a real thing, so prioritise the people you want to see and don't be afraid to say no," says Amy, founder of Social Cactus Coaching (www.social-cactus.com). Focus on spending time with the people who lift you, and when someone asks something of you, don't put yourself under undue pressure. "It's easy to promise something when we're in a good mood, so be mindful of what's realistic," adds Audrey. "It's better to say 'no' when someone has time to find an alternative."

EMBRACE THE OUTDOORS

It's tempting to hunker down by the fire, but spending just 20 minutes in nature can really lift your spirits, calming anxiety and lowering your levels of the stress hormone, cortisol. "Set a time each day when you'll all go out for a walk," says Audrey, author of *The Leader's Guide to Resilience* (Pearson, £14.99). "Immersing yourself in nature will give your mood such a boost." To up the ante, Audrey suggests playing this game. "Name five festive things you can see, four you can hear, three you can smell, two you can touch and one you can taste," she says. "It grounds you in the moment, helping you to feel calm and experience joy."

THE FIVE-MINUTE FIX

If family tensions or your to-do list threaten to overwhelm you, find a quiet space and do a five-minute breathing exercise. It may feel indulgent, but it'll pay dividends. "When you're stressed, your heart beats faster, the blood flows round your body quicker and you breathe more quickly," says Mark Newey, founder of www.headucate.me. "But if you take five minutes to consciously slow down your breath, you steady your heart rate and your brain wave activity too. This relaxes you and helps you feel more energised." Mark recommends breathing in for the count of four, holding your breath for four, then breathing out to the count of eight. In just five minutes, you'll calmer and in a better frame of mind to enjoy the day.

Appetisers & APERITIFS

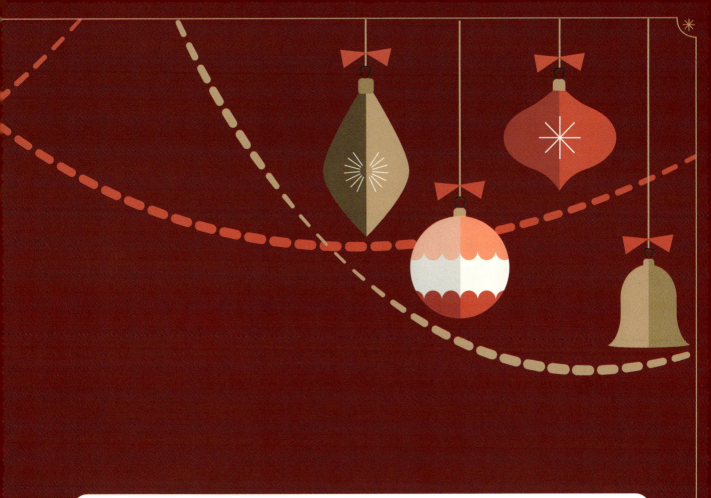

Lamb pitta bites

Spice things up with these parcels of lamb, infused with the flavours of north Africa. Very Moorish!

Makes 18 • Ready in 30 mins

- ✳ 250g | 8.8 fl oz minced lamb
- ✳ 4tsp ras el hanout
- ✳ 4tbsp chopped fresh mint, plus baby mint leaves for garnish
- ✳ 150g | 8.8 fl oz plain Greek yogurt
- ✳ 3 pitta breads
- ✳ ½tbsp sunflower or olive oil
- ✳ 1 small red onion, sliced, mixed with 1tbsp lemon juice
- ✳ seeds of ½ pomegranate

1 Mix together the lamb, ras el hanout, half the mint and a pinch of salt. Using lightly oiled hands, shape the mixture into 18 small patties, transfer to a plate, cover and chill until ready to cook. Stir the remaining mint into the yogurt and season.

2 Heat the grill to high. Split each pitta bread in half horizontally. Cut each half into 3 triangles and put on a baking tray. Grill for 1-2 mins on one side until golden and crisp.

3 When ready to serve, heat the oil in a non-stick frying pan. Add the lamb patties and fry for 2 mins on each side until cooked through.

4 Spoon a dollop of the yogurt mixture onto each pitta triangle, then add a lamb patty and some onion. Garnish with the baby mint leaves and pomegranate seeds.

Per serving of 3 canapes: 148 Cals, Fat 9.6g, Sat fat 4.2g, Carbs 10.2g

Courgette fritti with sweet dill sauce

A classic Italian-style finger food that will disappear quickly.

Serves 6 • Ready in 10 mins

- ✳ 2 large courgettes
- ✳ 50ml | 1.7 fl oz runny honey

TIP
Is your oil ready? Throw in a small chunk of bread. If it browns in 30 seconds, start cooking

- ✳ 50ml | 1.7 fl oz white wine vinegar
- ✳ 350ml | 12 fl oz sunflower oil
- ✳ 150g | 5.3 oz pack tempura batter, plus iced water to mix as per instructions
- ✳ pinch of Maldon salt
- ✳ small bunch fresh dill

YOU WILL NEED
- ✳ metal or heatproof tongs
- ✳ thick kitchen roll

1 Roughly slice the courgettes into chip-sized sticks and set aside.

2 Whisk the honey and vinegar together with a fork and set aside.

3 Meanwhile, gently heat 350ml sunflower oil in a deep pan until hot and starting to bubble lightly.

4 Mix up a 150g pack tempura batter mix according to the pack instructions. Dip the courgettes in the batter to coat, then gently shake off any excess and carefully place them into the hot oil, one by one. Fry for 2-3 mins until puffed, blistering and lightly golden then lift out with tongs and set aside on thick kitchen roll.

5 Season well with rock salt. Serve the courgette fritti warm, with the honey and vinegar and some shredded dill.

Per serving : Cals 198, Fat 11g, Sat fat 1.4g, Carbs 20g

Ham and chutney scones

The perfect classic tangy morsel.

Makes 20 • Ready in 30 mins

* **175g | 6 oz self-raising flour**
* **75g | 2.6 oz butter**
* **1tsp Dijon mustard**
* **5tbsp buttermilk**
* **100g | 3.5 oz ham hock**
* **1tsp fruit chutney**

1 Preheat oven to 220°C/425°F/ Gas Mark 7. Grease a baking sheet.
2 Mix together self-raising flour and butter in a food processor until fine breadcrumbs form. Add the Dijon mustard and buttermilk. Mix to form a dough. Turn out onto a floured surface and roll out to a 2cm thickness. Cut 4.5cm rounds. Place on a greased baking tray. Re-roll and use up trimmings. Bake for 12 mins until risen and golden. Cool on wire rack.
3 To serve, halve and butter the scones. Flake ham hock and pile onto scones and top each with fruit chutney.
Per serving: Cals 198, Fat 6.2g, Sat fat 3.6g, Carbs 26g

Roasted scallops on sticks

Fancier than a prawn for your classy canapé party.

Makes 12 • Ready in 20 mins

* **12 large scallops**
* **a little sunflower oil**
* **4 spring onions**
* **4tbsp sweet chilli sauce**
* **3tbsp chopped coriander**

1 Preheat oven to 200°C/400°F/ Gas Mark 6. Brush the scallops with a little oil and season with salt and pepper. Heat griddle pan and flash sear the scallops till the edges just turn golden. Transfer to roasting tin.
2 Bring small pan of water to boil. Halve 4 spring onions and shred each piece lengthways.
Cook for 2 mins. Drain and dry on kitchen paper.
3 Place the spring onion on top of scallops and cook in the oven for 10 mins.
4 Mix the sweet chilli sauce with the chopped coriander.
5 Transfer the scallops to a plate and spoon a little sauce onto each, skewer with cocktail sticks and serve.
Per serving: Cals 165, Fat 3.9g, Sat fat 1.2g, Carbs 6.2g

Hedgerow fizz

An essential on every good cocktail menu and now you can make it from the comfort of your home.

Serves 6 • Ready in 15 mins

* **175g | 6 oz blackberries**
* **50g | 1.7 oz caster sugar**
* **6tbsp brandy**
* **1 bottle Champagne, chilled**

1 Heat the blackberries and caster sugar in a pan until the sugar has dissolved, simmer for 5 mins until thick and syrupy. Make sure you stir it occasionally.
2 Sieve into a bowl, pressing the fruit with the back of a spoon. Discard the fruit pulp and chill the syrup.
3 Mix the brandy with the blackberry syrup and pour a couple of tablespoons of this into each Champagne flute.
4 Pour the bottle of chilled Champagne, dividing it evenly between 6 glasses and serve to guests immediately.
Per serving: Cals 193, Fat 0g, Sat fat 0g, Carbs 25g

TIP
You can use frozen berries if you cannot get your hands on fresh ones

Scotch quail eggs

These are a little more fiddly to make than their larger cousins but will seriously impress your guests.

Makes 12 • Ready in 45 mins

* 12 quail's eggs
* plain flour, for dusting
* 400g | 14 oz sausage meat
* 1tsp fennel seeds, lightly crushed
* ½tsp cumin seeds, lightly crushed
* 1 red chilli, deseeded and finely chopped
* 3tbsp chopped parsley
* 1 egg, beaten
* 75g | 2.6 oz breadcrumbs
* vegetable oil, for frying

1 Put the quail's eggs in a pan. Cover with cold water and bring to the boil. Reduce the heat and simmer for 2 mins. Drain, rinse in cold water and peel. Roll the eggs in the flour to dust.

2 Mix the sausage meat in a bowl with the fennel, cumin, chilli, parsley and some seasoning until evenly combined. Divide into 12. Take a piece of sausage meat and flatten it out with your fingers to about 5mm thick. Use to wrap around an egg, pinching the edges together so the egg is enclosed, and roll in the palms of your hands.

3 Repeat with all the eggs. Dust with flour, then coat in the beaten egg and breadcrumbs.

4 Heat a 5cm depth of oil in a frying pan until a piece of bread turns golden in 1 min.

5 Cook the eggs in batches, lowering into the pan and frying for 5 mins until pale golden. If the breadcrumbs brown quickly, lower the heat so they don't over-cook. Serve warm or cold, cut in half.
Per serving: Cals 136, Fat 12g, Sat fat 7g, Carbs 2g

TIP
If you peel the eggs in cold water with a dash of vinegar, it makes the shells easier to remove

Watercress soup with smoked trout

The contrast of the pink trout against the green soup will have them oohing and aahing.

Makes 1 litre (enough to fill about 10 espresso cups)
• Ready in 30 mins

- ✳ **50g | 1.7 oz lightly salted butter**
- ✳ **3 shallots, roughly chopped**
- ✳ **2 medium potatoes, peeled and diced**
- ✳ **1 litre vegetable stock**
- ✳ **250g | 8.8 oz watercress, roughly chopped, tough stalks removed**
- ✳ **5tbsp crème fraiche**
- ✳ **75g | 2.6 oz smoked trout fillets**

1 Melt the butter in a pan and gently fry the shallots for 5 mins. Add the potatoes and stock, and bring to the boil. Reduce the heat and simmer for 15 mins or until the potatoes are tender.
2 Add the watercress and cook for 1 min, then whizz with a stick blender until smooth. Stir in the crème fraiche and season. To serve, pour into small cups. Shred the trout and place on top.
Per serving: Cals 239, Fat 6.2g, Sat fat 3.9g, Carbs 8.9g

TIP
Chill the soup as soon you make it to retain the vibrant colour

Baby roasted potatoes with herb salt

Guests will love this flavoursome salt.

Serves 8 • Ready in 1 hr 10 mins

- ✳ **500g | 17 oz new potatoes**
- ✳ **2tbsp olive oil**
- ✳ **2tbsp crushed pink peppercorns**
- ✳ **2tbsp each of chopped thyme,**
  parsley and chives
- ✳ **40g | 1.3 oz sea salt**

1 Preheat the oven to 200°C/400°F/Gas Mark 6. Toss the potatoes in the oil and roast for 1 hr or until golden, turning twice during cooking.
2 Mix together the remaining ingredients and place in a small dish.
3 Serve the potatoes with cocktail sticks for dipping into the herby salt.
Per serving: Cals 131, Fat 2.6g, Sat fat 1.3g, Carbs 26g

Melon and posh ham bites

A winning combo – and so simple.

Makes 20 • Ready in 10 mins

✴ **1 melon**
✴ **10 slices of Serrano ham**

1 Cut the melon into chunks and wrap each piece in half a slice of serrano ham.
Per serving: Cals 15, Fat 0.2g, Sat fat 0.2g, Carbs 1.3g

Bloody Mary gazpacho

Not keen on cold soup? Try this version which packs a boozy punch and helps clean your palate for the next snack – you'll be addicted!

Makes 6 • Ready in 10 mins, plus chilling

✴ **500g | 17 oz ripe tomatoes, halved and deseeded**
✴ **½tsp celery salt**
✴ **½ red chilli, sliced**
✴ a few sprigs of parsley, chopped
✴ freshly ground black pepper
✴ **50ml | 1.7 fl oz vodka**
✴ juice of ½ a lemon

YOU WILL NEED
✴ **6 shot glasses**

1 Blend all the ingredients together in a food processor until smooth. Chill before serving.
2 Fill the shot glasses with the soup.
Per serving: Cals 33, Fat 1.8g , Sat fat 0.9g, Carbs 12g

TIP
Garnish with small pieces of celery

USE A JAZZY COCKTAIL STICK TO KEEP THE HAM IN PLACE IF IT KEEPS SLIPPING OFF

Flaky goats' cheese biscuits

The dough for these freezes well.

Makes 40 • Ready in 25 mins, plus chilling

* 100g | 3.5 oz soft goats' cheese
* 3tbsp freshly grated Parmesan (or vegetarian alternative)
* 150g | 5.3 oz unsalted butter, softened
* ¼tsp cayenne pepper
* 175g | 6 oz plain flour

YOU WILL NEED

* 3 baking trays lined with baking parchment, and cookie cutters

1 Put the goats' cheese, 2tbsp of the Parmesan, the butter and the cayenne pepper in a food processor and blitz until smooth. Add the flour and blitz again until just combined. Wrap the dough in clingfilm and leave to chill in the fridge for around 2hrs, until firm.
2 Heat the oven to 180°C/350°F/ Gas Mark 4. Remove the dough from the fridge and roll out to a 2cm-thick oblong. Using the cookie cutters, cut out 40 biscuits and lay them on the baking trays. Sprinkle the remaining Parmesan on top of the biscuits and bake for 10-12mins, until golden brown. Transfer the biscuits to a wire rack to cool. These can be stored in an airtight container for 3-4 days.
Per biscuit: Cals 57, Fat 4g, Sat fat 2.5g, Carbs 3.5g

Crostini with onion marmalade and blue cheese

Slice a small baguette into rounds, drizzle with olive oil and bake in a hot oven until crisp. Alternatively, buy ready-made crostini. Top the crostini with onion marmalade and a little blue cheese.

Hot potato skins

Heat the oven to 220°C/425°F/ Gas Mark 7. Scrub 6 potatoes, prick all over with a fork and bake in the oven for 1hr. Cut each into 6-8 wedges. Scoop out the centre of each wedge, leaving 1cm of potato behind in each skin. Put the skins, cut-side up, on a baking tray, brush with olive oil and return them to the oven for 20-30mins, until almost golden. Serve with sour cream, guacamole or sweet chilli sauce. For a delicious red pepper mayo to dip the potato skins into, whizz together 6 Peppadew peppers with a small pot of fresh mayonnaise and a few drops of Tabasco sauce.

Crostini with onion marmalade and blue cheese

Flaky goats' cheese biscuits

Chicken and porcini mushroom vol-au-vents

Easily turn frozen vol-au-vent cases into moreish bites.

Makes 60 · Ready in 30 mins

- ✳ 40g | **1.3 oz dried porcini mushrooms**
- ✳ 350g | **13 oz cooked chicken**
- ✳ **6tbsp chicken stock**
- ✳ 200ml | **7 fl oz double cream**
- ✳ 50g | **1.7 oz Parmesan, grated, plus a few shavings, to decorate**
- ✳ **1 bunch of fresh tarragon**
- ✳ **60 frozen mini vol-au-vent cases**
- ✳ **1 egg, beaten**

1 Heat the oven to 200°C/400°F/ Gas Mark 6. Soak the porcini mushrooms in 250ml boiling water for 15 mins. Drain, reserving 4tbsp of the liquid. Roughly chop the mushrooms, transfer to a non-stick frying pan and sauté for 2-3 mins. Add the liquid and cook for 1-2 mins. Remove from the heat and leave to cool.
2 In a large bowl, shred the chicken into small pieces, then add the mushrooms, stock, cream and Parmesan. Chop most of the tarragon, keeping some leaves whole for decoration. Stir the chopped tarragon through the chicken mixture and season.
3 Glaze the edges of the pastry cases with egg and bake for 6-7 mins until golden brown. Leave to cool slightly on a wire rack. Then, squash in the middle of the vol-au-vents with your finger, and spoon 1tsp of the filling into each case. Top each vol-au-vent with tarragon leaves or Parmesan shavings to serve.
Per vol-au-vent: Cals 84, Fat 6g, Sat fat 3g, Carbs 5g

Glam sausage rolls

Always a party favourite!

Makes 18 · Ready in 50 mins

- ✳ **18 cocktail sausages**
- ✳ 500g | **17 oz block puff pastry**
- ✳ **1 egg, beaten**
- ✳ **a few sesame and poppy seeds**

1 Heat the oven to 180°C/350°F/ Gas Mark 4. Put the sausages on an oiled baking tray and bake for 15-20 mins, until cooked. Remove from the oven and leave to cool.
2 Roll out the pastry to 3mm thick and roughly 30x15cm wide. Cut into 18 x 7cm squares. Brush the egg over the pastry squares and place a sausage diagonally across each. Fold over the opposite corners of the square and pinch together to seal. Brush over a little more egg, then sprinkle over some seeds. Put on a baking tray and bake for 15-20 mins, until golden. Serve warm.
Per serving: Cals 149, Fat 10g, Sat fat 4g, Carbs 22g

*So flash, yet so simple – these little bites
are the perfect cocktail party nibble*

Smoked salmon canapés

**Shop-bought blinis and crispy
granary toasts cut into star shapes
make attractive bases
for these posh toppings.**

Makes 40 · Ready in 10 mins

* 6 slices granary bread
* 16 blinis
* 200ml | 7 fl oz crème fraîche
* 150g | 5.3 oz garlic and herb
  cream cheese (such as Boursin)
* 200g | 7 oz smoked salmon
* 80g | 3.5 oz lumpfish caviar
* several sprigs of fresh dill

1 Lightly toast the bread. Then, using
a biscuit cutter, stamp 4 stars out of
each slice, or trim off the crusts and
cut each slice into quarters.
2 In a bowl, stir together 3tbsp
of the crème fraîche with the garlic
and herb cream cheese.
3 Spoon this mixture on top of the
blinis and top each with a twirl of
smoked salmon and a sprig of dill.
4 Top each toast with a piece of
salmon, a dollop of crème fraîche
and ½tsp caviar.
*Per blini: Cals 63, Fat 4g,
Sat fat 2g, Carbs 4g*

Jewelled hazelnut couscous

Perfect for when you need some respite from all those classic Christmas dishes.

Serves 6 • Ready in 15 mins

* **350g | 12 oz Belazu barley couscous**
* **1tsp ground cumin**
* **1tsp ground coriander**
* **700ml | 24 fl hot vegetable stock**
* **6tbsp olive oil**
* **3tbsp pomegranate molasses**
* **4tbsp tomato purée**
* **100g | 3.5 oz hazelnuts, chopped**
* **100g | 3.5 oz walnuts, chopped**
* **2tbsp chopped fresh coriander**
* **2tbsp chopped fresh parsley**
* **pomegranate seeds, to decorate**

1 Put the couscous in a large bowl with the ground cumin and coriander, and pour over the stock. Cover the bowl with clingfilm and leave until all the liquid has been absorbed.
2 Mix in the remaining ingredients and season to taste. This recipe is also delicious made with rice instead of the couscous.
Per serving: Cals 580, Fat 34g, Sat fat 4g, Carbs 52g

Garlicky jackets

Irresistible buffet food!

Makes 20 • Ready in 1hr

* **20 small potatoes**
* **100g | 3.5 oz butter, softened**
* **2 garlic cloves, crushed**
* **1tbsp chopped fresh parsley**

1 Using a melon baller, scoop a hole from the top of each potato.
2 Mix together the butter, garlic and parsley, form into a log shape and wrap in clingfilm. Leave in the fridge to firm up, then top each potato with a chunk of the garlic butter. Heat the oven to 200°C/400°F/ Gas Mark 6. Roast the potatoes for 45mins and serve immediately.
Per serving: Cals 105, Fat 4g, Sat fat 2.5g, Carbs 14g

TIP
You could fully bake the bread ahead of time, then melt the Brie in its box separately, returning the bread to the oven to warm through for 5mins

For a truly indulgent sharing plate, pair the rich flavours of Brie and pesto with a good bottle of red

Tear-and-share pesto bread with melted Brie

Herby bread ready to dunk into delicious melted cheese – perfect!

Serves 8-10 • Ready in 1hr 30 mins, plus rising and proving

* **150ml | 5.3 fl oz milk**
* **420g | 14.5 oz strong white flour**
* **1½tsp fast-action dried yeast**
* **1tsp sugar**
* **1tsp sea salt**
* **5 prunes and 5 dried apricots**
* **1kg | 2.2 lb Petit Brie, Brie de Nangis or Le Rustique Camembert in a box (make sure you use a veggie cheese if serving veggies)**

FOR THE PESTO
* **1 large garlic clove**
* **25g | 0.8 oz each fresh parsley and basil**
* **100g | 3.5 oz pine nuts**
* **80ml | 3 fl oz olive oil**
* **juice of ½ lemon**
* **you will need**
* **a 20cm-round cake tin, the outside oiled, and a large, oiled baking tray**

1 First, make the dough. Gently heat the milk with 150ml water. In a large bowl, mix together the flour, yeast, sugar and salt. Stir in the milk mixture. Knead the dough in a mixer with a dough hook, or by hand on a floured surface for about 10mins until soft and springy. Transfer the dough to an oiled bowl and cover with a sheet of oiled clingfilm. Leave in a warm place, until doubled in size.
2 Meanwhile, make the pesto. Use a food processor or a pestle and mortar to blitz the garlic, herbs, most of the pine nuts, the oil and lemon juice to a pesto consistency. Spoon into a small bowl.
3 Once the bread has risen, turn it out onto a floured surface and knock it back with your hands. Then roll it into a rectangle about 60cm long. Spread the pesto over the dough and carefully roll it up.
4 Place the oiled cake tin in the centre of the oiled baking tray (or oven tray). Cut the bread into 2.5cm-thick slices and arrange cut-side up around the tin. They don't need to touch as the bread will rise and expand. Scatter over the remaining pine nuts, cover with more oiled clingfilm and leave to prove until doubled in size.
5 Heat the oven to 200°C/400°F/ Gas Mark 6. Scatter sea salt over the bread and bake for 25mins. Meanwhile, stud the dried fruit into the Brie. Carefully lift the cake tin out from the centre of the bread and replace with the Brie. Return to the oven for another 20-25mins until the bread has risen and browned, and the cheese is soft and melted. Serve warm.
Per serving: Cals 722-577g, Fat 44-36g, Sat fat 20-16g, Carbs 44-35g

Falafels with green goddess dressing

For a healthier twist, bake the falafels (200°C/400°F/Gas Mark 6) with a drizzle of olive oil for 30 mins. These are vegan without dressing, or using vegan alternatives.

Makes 15 • Ready in 45 mins, plus soaking and chilling

- 250g | 8.8 oz dried chickpeas, soaked overnight in 500ml | 17 fl oz of cold water
- 1 small onion, finely chopped
- 1 garlic clove, crushed
- 2tbsp coriander, finely chopped
- 1tbsp parsley, finely chopped, plus extra leaves to garnish
- ¼tsp cayenne pepper
- 2tsp garam masala
- 1tsp baking powder
- 1½tbsp gram flour
- sesame seeds, to coat
- sunflower oil, to fry

FOR THE DRESSING

- 200ml | 7 fl oz mayonnaise (or vegan mayo)
- 1tsp capers, rinsed and finely chopped
- 1 small bunch chives, chopped
- 1 small bunch parsley, roughly chopped
- A few sprigs of tarragon, leaves only, roughly chopped
- 1 garlic clove, crushed
- 50ml | 1.7 fl oz crème fraîche or soured cream (or vegan crème fraîche)
- Tabasco and lemon juice, to serve

1 Heat the oven to 140°C/275°F/ Gas Mark 1. Drain the chickpeas and mix well with the onion, garlic, coriander and parsley. Put a third of the mixture into a food processor and pulse until it's finely chopped and starts to hold itself together, then transfer to a bowl. Don't over-blend as it will become gluey. Repeat for the remaining mixture.
2 Add the spices, baking powder and flour, season well. Use your hands to mix, then cover and chill for at least 1 hr, or until ready to shape.
3 To make the dressing, blitz all the ingredients in a food processor until mostly broken up and a bright green colour. Season if necessary. Set aside.
4 With slightly wet hands, shape a heaped tbsp of the falafel mixture into a small patty, then roll in sesame seeds and put on a baking tray lined with baking parchment until ready to cook. Repeat until you have 15 falafels.
5 Fill a deep, wide pan with 2.5cm of oil and heat over a medium heat until a small piece of bread browns in 30-40 secs, then fry the falafels in batches for 10 mins or until crisp and golden brown, turning occasionally.
6 Drain on kitchen paper, then arrange on a platter with the dressing. Garnish with parsley leaves and serve.
Per serving: Cals 200, Fat 16.5g, Sat Fat 2.9g, Carbs 10g

Fondue with herby potatoes

A really good filler for a small drinks party.

Serves 8 • Ready in 30 mins

✳ **750g | 26 oz baby new potatoes**
✳ **2tbsp olive oil**
✳ **3 sprigs of thyme**
✳ **100g | 3.5 oz Comté, grated**
✳ **100g | 3.5 oz Gruyère, grated**
✳ **100g | 3.5 oz Emmental, grated**
✳ **2tsp cornflour**
✳ **1 garlic clove**
✳ **350ml | 12 fl oz dry white wine**
✳ **Small glass of Calvados or kirsch**

1 Heat the oven to 200°C/400°F/ Gas Mark 6. Tip the potatoes into a large roasting tin, drizzle over olive oil and toss with the thyme and pinch of sea salt. Roast for 20-25 mins until cooked through and golden.
2 Meanwhile, mix together the cheese and cornflour. Rub the base of a pan with the garlic then discard. Add the wine to the pan and heat until simmering gently. The trick is to add the cheese gradually, stirring all the time – like making risotto. As it melts, add another handful of cheese. Once all the cheese has been incorporated and the mixture has thickened, stir in the Calvados. Serve as a dip with the potatoes.
Per serving: Cals 302, Fat 15g, Sat Fat 8g, Carbs 18g

TIP
If you're in a pinch, use ready-cooked beetroot as a time saving hack.

Spicy beetroot dip

Beetroot's earthiness lends itself well to the spices in this dip.

Serves 6 • Ready in 1 hr 35 mins

✳ **600g | 21 oz bunched beetroot**
✳ **1 red onion, peeled and cut into wedges**
✳ **2tbsp olive oil**
✳ **1tsp cumin seeds**
✳ **1tsp fennel seeds**
✳ **¼tsp mild chilli powder**
✳ **Small bunch mint, roughly chopped**
✳ **100ml | 3.5 fl oz Greek yogurt**

1 Heat the oven to 200°C/400°F/ Gas Mark 6. Trim and peel the beetroot and cut into small wedges. Scatter in a roasting tin with the onion and drizzle with the oil. Sprinkle over the cumin, fennel and chilli powder. Cover with foil and bake for 1 hr 15 mins or until the vegetables are tender. Leave to cool for 10 mins.
2 Tip into a food processor and add the mint and a little salt. Blend until puréed, scraping down any lumps that cling to the sides of the bowl. Add the yogurt and blend in. Check the seasoning and turn into a serving bowl. Serve with flatbreads.
Per serving: Cals 90, Fat 5g, Sat Fat 1g, Carbs 9g

Pea and paneer fritters

Yummy little morsels that are sweet and spicy with an added crunch.

Makes 20 • Ready in 10 mins

* 1 egg
* Squeeze of fresh lemon juice
* 3tbsp plain flour
* ¼tsp baking powder
* ¼tsp garam masala
* 100g | 3.5 oz peas, half puréed

* 75g | 2.6 oz paneer cheese, diced
* 1tsp sunflower oil
* 4 fresh kaffir lime leaves (optional), sliced into 10 strips
* Handful of mini poppadoms
* 2-3tbsp Greek yoghurt
* 1-2tbsp mango chutney

1 In a bowl, whisk together the egg, lemon juice, flour, baking powder and garam masala. Stir in the pea purée, remaining peas and paneer. 2 Fry teaspoonfuls of the mixture in a little oil for 2 mins until golden, then add the lime leaves to crisp them up. Serve each fritter topped with yoghurt, a piece of poppadum, mango chutney and the lime leaves.
Per serving: Cals 37, Fat 2g, Sat Fat 1g, Carbs 3g

Cauliflower 'Buffalo wings'

These will be a firm favourite at your next gathering!

Serves 4 • Ready in 30 mins

- ✳ **500ml | 17 fl oz oil, for frying**
- ✳ **1 large cauliflower, trimmed and cut into medium florets**
- ✳ **8tbsp plain flour**
- ✳ **1tbsp paprika**
- ✳ **2tsp ground white pepper**
- ✳ **2tbsp runny honey**
- ✳ **6tbsp hot sauce**
- ✳ **2tsp garlic salt**
- ✳ **Salad and chopped spring onions, to serve**

FOR THE DIP
- ✳ **150g | 5.3 oz blue cheese (we used Cashel Blue)**
- ✳ **4tbsp natural yogurt**
- ✳ **1tsp lemon juice**

1 To make the dip, blend the cheese, yogurt and lemon juice with black pepper until smooth, store in fridge until ready to serve.
2 Mix the flour, paprika and white pepper in a bowl. In another bowl, mix the honey, hot sauce and garlic salt. Roll the cauliflower in the flour mixture, a few at a time. Dip in the hot sauce, then coat again in the flour, set aside.
3 Fill a medium heavy-based pan with the oil to around 9cm deep and heat to 190°C/375°F, test by cooking a bit of cauliflower in it – it should start to brown in 20 secs, but take care not to overheat.
4 Fry the cauliflower for 1-2 mins until crispy. Keep warm in the oven while you cook the rest. Sprinkle with spring onions. Serve with the dip and salad.
Per serving: Cals 638, Fat 31g, Sat Fat 11g, Carbs 74g

Cheese, Marmite and sesame twists

Love it or hate it, savoury Marmite takes this party snack to the next level!

Makes 32 • Ready in 30 mins

✳ **3tsp Marmite**
✳ **500g | 10.5 oz block puff pastry**
✳ **150g | 5.3 oz Cheddar, grated**
✳ **1 egg, beaten**
✳ **2tbsp black sesame seeds**

1 Heat the oven to 220°C/425°F/ Gas Mark 7. Put the Marmite in a bowl and microwave for 15 secs, until runny.
2 Roll out the pastry to a large rectangle, about the thickness of a £1 coin. Spread the runny Marmite over half of the pastry and scatter the cheese on top. Fold down the other half of the pastry over the top.

Roll the filled pastry out again to a large rectangle. Brush over the egg and scatter over the sesame seeds.
3 Cut the pastry into ½cm-wide strips, then twist each strip and place on a lined baking tray. Bake in the oven for 15 mins, or until crisp and golden.
Per twist: Cals: 86, Fat 6g, Sat fat 3g, Carbs 5g

Cheesy tartlets

Our fave combo of cheese and tomato... and so easy to make!

Makes 20 • Ready in 25 mins

* **250g | 8.8 oz ready-rolled puff pastry (from a 375g pack)**
* **4tbsp spiced tomato chutney**
* **10 cherry tomatoes, quartered**
* **few sprigs thyme, leaves only**
* **150g | 5.3 oz soft goats' cheese, such as chèvre log, cut into pieces**

1 Heat oven to 200°C/400°F/ Gas Mark 6. Unroll pastry; using a lightly floured 6cm round, fluted cutter, cut out 20 discs. Transfer to two lightly oiled baking trays.
2 Using a fork, prick the surface of each round all over. Spread each with ½tsp chutney, add some tomatoes, thyme leaves and goats' cheese.
3 Chill until ready to bake (up to 6 hrs ahead). Bake for 10-15 mins until the pastry is golden and puffed up. Serve warm.
Per serving: Cals 75, Fat 5g, Sat Fat 3g, Carbs 5g

Baby rarebit bites

Mustardy cheese toasties that will be so hard to resist.

Makes 25 • Ready in 20 mins, plus chilling time

* **75ml dry cider**
* **1tbsp wholegrain mustard**
* **150g mature Cheddar, coarsely grated**
* **25g butter**
* **25g white breadcrumbs**
* **1 egg yolk, beaten**
* **1 seedy baguette, sliced into 25 x 1.5cm thick rounds**
* **2-3 spring onions, finely sliced**

1 Pour cider into a pan, bring to the boil, then simmer and reduce to 2tbsp. Add mustard, Cheddar and butter. Stir until cheese begins to melt. Remove from heat. Beat in breadcrumbs and egg yolk, season with black pepper. Leave to cool slightly.
2 Heat grill to medium-high. Grill baguette slices for 30 secs on each side until golden. When cool, spread with cheese mixture; grill for 2-3 mins. Top with spring onions to serve.
Per serving: Cals 72, Fat 3.5g, Sat Fat 2g, Carbs 7g

TIP
You can swap the pastry for mini-toasts – just grill rather than bake

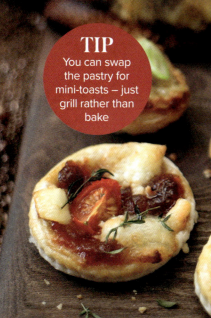

These small bites pair beautifully with our delicious winter cocktail recipes, overleaf

Beetroot blinis with garlicky mushrooms

Our beetroot and mushroom topping gives the usual smoked salmon blinis a veggie twist

Makes 30 • Ready in 50 mins

* 150g | 5.3 oz buckwheat flour
* 7g sachet easy blend yeast
* 250ml | 8.8 fl oz milk, gently warmed
* 2 medium eggs
* 25g | 0.8 oz melted butter, for frying

FOR THE TOPPING

* 150g | 5.3 oz cooked beetroot (not in vinegar)
* 3tbsp crème fraîche
* 125g | 4.4 oz ricotta cheese
* Small bunch dill, half roughly chopped
* 40g | 2.3 oz butter
* 250g | 8.8 oz button mushrooms, sliced
* 3 garlic cloves, finely chopped

1 Whisk together the flour, yeast, milk and eggs to make a smooth batter. Leave for 30 mins until frothy.

2 Heat a large frying pan over a medium heat, brush with a little of the melted butter and drop dessert spoonfuls of the batter into the pan, spaced about 5cm apart. Cook for about 1 min until set and golden underneath before turning and cooking for another minute. Repeat until all the batter is used.

3 In a food processor, whizz the beetroot, crème fraîche and ricotta together. Season, stir in the chopped dill and chill.

4 Melt the butter in a large frying pan, add the mushrooms and garlic and fry until the mushrooms are golden. To serve, warm the blinis for a few secs in the microwave, spread with a teaspoonful of beetroot mix and top with a few mushrooms and a small sprig of dill.

Per blini: Cals 57, Fat 3.5g, Sat Fat 2g, Carbs 5g

TIP
A small sprig of dill adds a wonderful depth of flavour to these blinis

Cinnamon and hazelnut martini

Aperol spritz

Pisco sour

Cheers!

Serve up a selection of refreshing cocktails at your festive occasion.

PISCO SOUR
Serves 2

✳ 100ml | 3.5 fl oz Pisco brandy or vodka
✳ juice of 2 limes
✳ 1½tbsp agave syrup
✳ 1 large egg white
✳ a few dashes of bitters

Place all the ingredients, apart from the bitters, into a cocktail shaker and shake well. Pour into glasses and top each with a dash of bitters.

APEROL SPRITZ
Serves 2

✳ 200ml | 7 fl oz Prosecco
✳ 100ml | 3.5 fl oz Aperol aperitif
✳ 50ml | 1.7 fl oz soda water
✳ slices of orange

Pour the Prosecco, Aperol and soda water into a tumbler or wine glass, and top with ice cubes and a slice of orange.

CINNAMON AND HAZELNUT MARTINI
Serves 2

✳ 50 ml | 1.7 fl oz vodka
✳ 50 ml | 1.7 fl oz Frangelico
✳ 50 ml | 1.7 fl oz espresso
✳ sprinkle of ground cinnamon

Mix together the vodka, Frangelico, espresso and ice, strain into a martini glass and sprinkle with cinnamon.

MULLED WHITE WINE
Makes a jug

Bottle of Riesling or Chardonnay
200ml | 7 fl oz clear apple juice
5 cloves
3cm root ginger, sliced
1 star anise
2 cinnamon sticks
3tbsp clear honey
2tbsp golden caster sugar
zest of 1 orange
75ml | 2.6 fl oz Calvados

Try our winter warming cocktails as a celebratory starter to a drinks party

Apple mojito

Passion fruit caipirinha

Mulled white wine

Place all the ingredients into a pan and bring to a gentle simmer, cover and remove from the heat. Set aside to infuse for 10-15mins. Serve warm.

APPLE MOJITO
Serves 2

* **75ml | 2.6 fl oz white rum**
* **zest and juice of 1 lime, plus extra lime wedges, to garnish**

* **175ml | 6 fl oz apple juice**
* **a large handful of mint leaves**
* **2tsp demerara sugar**
* **100ml | 3.5 fl oz soda water**
* **a few slices of apple, to garnish**

Shake all the ingredients, except for the soda water, in a cocktail shaker and pour over ice. Top with the soda water and garnish with an apple slice.

PASSION FRUIT CAIPIRINHA
Serves 2

* **juice and seeds of 1 passion fruit**
* **1tsp golden caster sugar**
* **1 lime, cut into small wedges**
* **a small handful of mint**
* **50ml | 1.7 fl oz Cachaça**
* **crushed ice**

Place all the ingredients into 2 tumblers with a small amount of ice and muddle until well combined. Top up with more crushed ice and serve.

TIP
Nothing says party quite like a cocktail. Give your guests the shaker and let them make their own!

Whisky royale

Whisky adds a touch of old-school elegance to the cocktail selection.

Makes 1 • Ready in 5 mins

* 45ml | 1.5 fl oz (3tbsp) whisky
* 30ml | 1 fl oz (2tbsp) ginger syrup (from a jar of stem ginger)
* 75ml | 2.6 fl oz fresh apple juice
* plenty of ice
* twist of lemon peel

Pour all the ingredients (except the lemon twist) into a cocktail shaker or jug. Shake together then strain into a Martini glass and add a twist of lemon peel.

Boulevardier

A drink that's served with a Christmassy twist.

Makes 1 • Ready in 5 mins

* plenty of ice
* 30 ml | 1 fl oz (2tbsp) bourbon
* 30 ml | 1 fl oz (2tbsp) white vermouth
* 30 ml | 1 fl oz (2tbsp) red vermouth
* maraschino cherry
* twist of orange peel

Fill a whisky tumbler with some ice. Pour in the bourbon, white vermouth and red vermouth. Stir well, then add a maraschino cherry and a twist of orange peel.

Lime spritz

Gin is in vogue at the moment so your line-up must include this!

Makes 1 • Ready in 5 mins

* plenty of ice
* 30ml | 1 fl oz (2tbsp) gin
* juice and zest of 1 lime

* 15ml | 0.5 fl oz (1tbsp) elderflower cordial
* tonic water
* long twist of cucumber

Put the ice into a tumbler. Add the gin, lime juice and zest, elderflower cordial and top up with tonic. Stir well and add the cucumber twist.

Winter sidecar

Clementine juice will add festive cheer to this classic cocktail.

Makes 1 • Ready in 5 mins

* 15ml | 0.5 fl oz (1tbsp) clementine juice (available at M&S)
* cinnamon sugar
* 45ml | 1.5 fl oz (3tbsp) brandy
* 30ml | 1 fl oz (2tbsp) white vermouth
* plenty of ice

Moisten the rim of a cocktail glass with a little clementine juice, then dip into a small plate of cinnamon sugar and set aside. Shake together 15ml clementine juice, the brandy and the white vermouth in a shake with the ice and strain into the glass.

Cramaretto sour

This mix of drinks with cranberry is simply delicious.

Makes 1 • Ready in 5 mins

* 45 ml | 1.5 fl oz (3tbsp) vodka
* 30 ml | 1 oz (2tbsp) Amaretto
* 100 ml | 3.5 fl oz cranberry juice
* plenty of ice
* a few fresh cranberries

Mix together all the ingredients (except the cranberries) in a shaker with the ice. Strain into a cocktail glass, then top with the cranberries.

Frozen cranberries work well too and can help to chill the drink

KEEP THE JAR OF MARASCHINO CHERRIES IN THE FRIDGE AFTER GARNISHING WITH THEM

TIP
You could use lime cordial in place of elderflower to make an even purer lime spritz

Soups & STARTERS

Butternut squash soup

Avoid the cold weather and curl up with a bowl of this creamy squash soup.

Serves 6 • Ready in 40 mins

- ✶ **1tbsp rapeseed oil**
- ✶ **1 onion, chopped**
- ✶ **2tsp ground coriander**
- ✶ **750 g | 1.6 lb butternut squash, deseeded and cubed**
- ✶ **2 medium-sized sweet potatoes, cubed**
- ✶ **1.75 litres vegetable stock (gluten-free if needed)**
- ✶ **150 ml | 5 fl oz soured cream**
- ✶ **1tsp crushed pink peppercorns**

1 Heat the oil in a large pan. Add the onion and fry gently for 5 mins, to soften. Add the ground coriander and cook for 1-2 mins. Add the cubed butternut squash and sweet potatoes and pour in the vegetable stock. Bring to the boil and simmer for 20 mins, until the vegetables are tender.
2 Pour the soup, in batches, into a blender and whizz until smooth. (You can prepare this a couple of days in advance, and chill in an airtight container.)
3 To serve, warm the soup through thoroughly and swirl in the soured cream and add a sprinkling of crushed pink peppercorns.
Per serving: Cals 200, Fat 7g, Sat fat 3g, Carbs 26g

Celeriac, Camembert and truffle soup with thyme

This luxuriously rich soup is bound to impress even the fussiest dinner guests.

Serves 8 • Ready in 1 hr 15 mins

- ✶ **25 g | 0.9 oz butter**
- ✶ **1 large onion, chopped**
- ✶ **300 g | 10.5 oz King Edward or Desiree potatoes, peeled and chopped**
- ✶ **2 celeriac, around 1kg in total, peeled and chopped**
- ✶ **1 litre vegetable stock (gluten-free if needed)**
- ✶ **250 g | 8.8 oz ripe Camembert**
- ✶ **1 small black truffle, finely sliced (or use good truffle oil)**

1 Melt the butter and cook the onion very gently for around 10 mins, until soft. Add the potatoes and celeriac with plenty of seasoning, mix in well and cook for 5 mins. Add the stock, bring to the boil then simmer for around 45 mins, until the vegetables are soft and cooked through.
2 Blend to a purée. Get ahead: You can now freeze it or it will keep in the fridge for up to 2 days.
3 Cut the Camembert into wedges. Reheat the soup and divide between the bowls, then top with the cheese and truffle, or drizzle over the truffle oil.
Per serving: Cals 193, fat 10g, Sat Fat 6g, Carbs 12g

Thai spiced pumpkin soup

The flavourful toppings make this soup a bit more special.

Serves 6 • Ready in 1 hr 25 mins

- ✳ **650 g | 1.4 lb pumpkin, peeled, deseeded and diced**
- ✳ **2tbsp groundnut/sunflower oil**
- ✳ **4 small Thai shallots or 2 normal shallots**
- ✳ **A thumb-sized piece of fresh ginger, peeled and finely sliced**
- ✳ **2 lemongrass sticks, trimmed and sliced**
- ✳ **2 red chillies: 1 deseeded and roughly chopped; 1 finely sliced**
- ✳ **2 garlic cloves**
- ✳ **400 ml | 13.5 fl oz light coconut milk**
- ✳ **400 ml | 13.5 fl oz vegetable stock (gluten-free if needed)**
- ✳ **Light soy sauce, ground black pepper and lime juice, to taste**

TO SERVE
- ✳ **A handful of cashew nuts, toasted and crushed**
- ✳ **Small handful coriander sprigs**
- ✳ **2tbsp crispy fried shallots**

1 Heat the oven to 200°C/400°F/Gas Mark 6. Toss the pumpkin with the oil, shallots, ginger, lemongrass, roughly chopped chilli and garlic cloves in a roasting tin. Cover tightly with foil and roast for 1 hr, until very tender.

2 Tip half the pumpkin into a blender with the coconut milk and blitz until very smooth. Pour into a large saucepan. Blitz the remaining pumpkin mixture with the vegetable stock. Add this to the first batch and stir well.

3 Put the pan over a low heat and gently bring to the boil, stirring often. Simmer gently for 5 mins then season to taste with the soy sauce, black pepper and lime juice.

4 Divide the soup between warmed bowls and scatter with the toasted cashews, coriander sprigs, sliced chilli and crispy fried shallots (if using) just before eating.

Per serving: Cals 190, Fat 13g, Sat fat 6g, Carbs 13g

Herby fennel and cannellini bean soup with ricotta

This has got to be one of the most delicate, fragrant soups, but it also packs in lots of flavour.

Serves 6 • Ready in 45 mins

- ✳ **2tbsp olive oil, plus extra to drizzle**
- ✳ **1 large onion, sliced**
- ✳ **2 garlic cloves, sliced**
- ✳ **3 medium fennel bulbs, cut into wedges, fronds reserved**
- ✳ **½tsp crushed chillies**
- ✳ **1.5 litres vegetable stock**
- ✳ **2 x 400 g | 14 oz cans cannellini beans, rinsed and drained**
- ✳ **6tbsp ricotta**
- ✳ **Grated zest of ½ lemon**
- ✳ **4 dill sprigs, torn**
- ✳ **Sourdough toasts, to serve (gluten-free toast if required)**

1 Heat the oil in a large pan over a medium heat. Add the onion, garlic, fennel and a pinch of the crushed chillies. Season, stir to combine and cook with the lid on for 15 mins, stirring occasionally.

2 Pour in the stock and beans. Bring to the boil and simmer gently for 10-15 mins, or until fennel and onion are tender. Taste for seasoning. Just before serving, add the dill and reserved fennel fronds to pan, keeping a little of each for garnish.

3 Spoon into bowls and top with ricotta, a grating of lemon zest, a scattering of chilli, fennel fronds and dill and a drizzle of olive oil. Serve with sourdough toasts.

Per serving: Cals 200, fat 8g, Sat Fat 2g, Carbs 19g

TIP
Omit the ricotta
to make this
suitable for
vegans

Chunky savoy cabbage and potato soup broth

Celebrate the flavour of these humble ingredients with this deliciously delicate broth.

Serves 4 • Ready in 40 mins

✳ 1.5 litres vegetable stock (gluten-free if needed)
✳ 2 bay leaves
✳ 8 black peppercorns
✳ 2 celery sticks, sliced
✳ 2 carrots, scrubbed and thickly sliced the diagonal
✳ 2 onions, peeled and cut into thin wedges
✳ Zest of 1 lemon (½ pared, ½ grated)
✳ Salt
✳ 4 medium potatoes, peeled and finely chopped
✳ 1 small savoy cabbage, cut into wedges
✳ 1 garlic clove, peeled and finely chopped
✳ 4tbsp finely chopped flat-leaf parsley

1 Pour the stock into a large pan with the bay leaves, peppercorns, celery, carrot, onion and pared lemon zest. Simmer for 15 mins. Add salt to taste, then lower in the potatoes and simmer very gently for 10 mins. Add the cabbage.
2 Cook until the cabbage and potatoes are tender, about 6-8 mins. Stir in the garlic, parsley and grated lemon and serve with toasted sourdough and some English mustard to add a kick.
Per serving: Cals 300, Fat 1g, Sat Fat 0.5g, Carbs 56g

TIP
Garlic has long been hailed as an ancient superfood for helping fight infections. Garlic oil, meanwhile, has been shown to aid recovery from heart conditions

Roasted sweet garlic and almond soup

Roasting the garlic really brings out its natural sweetness

Serves: 4 • Ready in 1 hr

- **3 large bulbs fresh garlic, broken up, skins left on**
- **1 medium white onion, finely chopped**
- **4tbsp extra virgin olive oil**
- **285ml | 10.5 fl oz single cream**
- **1 litre organic vegetable stock**
- **1 large ciabatta loaf**
- **2tbsp sherry or white wine vinegar**
- **150g | 5.3 oz toasted flaked almonds**
- **pea shoots, to garnish**
- **sourdough, charred (optional)**

1 Heat the oven to 180°C/350°F/Gas Mark 4. Roast the garlic cloves for 30 mins until soft. Meanwhile, in a large pan, slowly fry the onion in the oil for 10 mins until soft and translucent. Add the cream and stock, bring to the boil and simmer for 10 mins. When cooked, allow the garlic to cool slightly. Squeeze out the pulp and whisk it into the soup.

2 Remove the crusts from the ciabatta, rip the bread up into small pieces and add to the soup. Add the vinegar, then allow the soup to simmer for 5 more mins. Blend in a food processor until smooth. Add the almonds, reserving some, and whizz again. Season to taste, garnish with almond and pea shoots, and serve with charred sourdough, if using.
Per serving: Cals 738, Fat 49g, Sat Fat 13g, Carbs 48g

Red chicory, walnut and goats' cheese salad

This warm, wintry salad is perfect for a lighter supper over the Christmas season.

Serves 4 • Ready in 20 mins

✴ 2tbsp olive oil
✴ 2 handfuls walnuts
✴ 3 heads red chicory, leaves separated
✴ 400 g | 14 oz goats' cheese, broken into chunks
✴ 6 sprigs thyme, leaves removed
✴ 3tbsp white wine vinegar
✴ 6tbsp walnut oil
✴ Pinch of sugar

1 Heat a frying pan with the olive oil, then add the walnuts with some sea salt and cook, tossing, for 3-4 mins until toasted and crisp. Allow to cool slightly, then divide the chicory, goats' cheese and thyme leaves between plates, and scatter the walnuts over.
2 Mix the vinegar, walnut oil and sugar, season and drizzle over the salads.
Per serving: Cals 612, fat 57g, Sat Fat 21g, Carbs 3g

Med-style potted goats' cheese

A fab alternative to a meat pâté, and the yummy olive toasts are the perfect crunchy foil!

Serves: 6 · Ready in 15 mins

* **1 loaf olive bread**
* **1 clove of garlic, crushed**
* **2tbsp extra virgin olive oil**
FOR THE POTTED CHEESE
* **300 g | 10.5 oz soft goats' cheese**
* **100g | 3.5 oz extra light soft cheese**

* **A little basil, chopped, plus leaves to garnish**
* **50 g | 1.7 oz sundried tomatoes in oil, drained and chopped**
* **50 g | 1.7 oz pitted black olives, chopped**
* **2tbsp capers, chopped**

1 Heat oven to 150°C/300°F/ Gas Mark 2. Thinly slice the bread and lay on a baking tray. Mix the garlic with 1tbsp oil and season. Brush a little on the bread and bake for 10-15 mins until crisp and golden.

Cool and store in an airtight container.
2 For the potted cheese, mix together all the ingredients (reserving a few tomatoes, olives, capers and basil leaves to garnish). Season, spoon into ramekins and chill. To serve, drizzle with the remaining oil and add the garnishes. Serve with the toasts.
Per serving: Cals 397, Fat 29g, Sat Fat 15g, Carbs 29g

Brie and sweet onion tarts

What's not to love about these sweet and savoury little tarts?

Makes 6 • Ready in 50 mins

* 2tbsp olive oil
* 3 large sweet onions, peeled and thinly sliced
* Few sprigs thyme, leaves only
* 375g | 13.2 oz pack ready-rolled puff pastry
* 1 egg, beaten
* 2tbsp redcurrant jelly
* 200g | 7 oz firm Brie, sliced
* 100g | 3.5 oz pack winter salad leaves

FOR THE DRESSING
* 2tsp Dijon mustard
* 3tbsp olive oil
* 2tbsp lemon juice
* Pinch of sugar

1 Add the olive oil, onions and most of the thyme to a large pan. Gently cook over a low heat for about 30-40 mins until onions are very soft and light golden. Stir often, so they don't catch, season well and leave to cool.
2 Preheat the oven to 190°C/375°F/Gas Mark 5. Unroll the pastry and cut out six rounds, each one 11cm in diameter. Transfer to a lightly greased baking tray, brush with beaten egg and prick with a fork, leaving a 1.5cm border unpricked around the edge. Spread the centre of each round with onion, then add a few little blobs of redcurrant jelly (about 1tsp each) into the middle.
3 Bake for 15 mins, then remove from the oven. Add a few slices of Brie, scatter over remaining thyme leaves and bake again for 10 mins.
4 To make the dressing, whisk all the ingredients together, then chill until required. Remove the tarts from the oven and cool for a few mins before serving with the salad leaves and a drizzle of dressing.
Per serving: Cals 500, fat 35g, Sat Fat 15g, Carbs 32g

Red rice and roots

A deliciously earthy salad, great as a starter or as a side dish.

Serves 4 • Ready in 2 hrs 30 mins

* 500 g | 17.6 oz uncooked beetroot
* 150 g | 5.3 oz Camargue red rice
* Grated zest and juice of 1 orange
* 2tbsp olive oil
* 2tbsp shelled pistachios, roughly chopped
* 100 g | 3.5 oz feta, crumbled
* Good handful of mint leaves, roughly chopped/torn or whole

1 Set the oven to 180°C/350°F/Gas Mark 4. Trim the beetroot, leaving a little bit of stalk on them, and put them in a roasting tin. Cover loosely with foil and bake for about 1½-2 hrs, depending on size, until tender.
2 Meanwhile, add rice to a pan of boiling water and simmer for 30 mins. Drain and cool.
3 While still warm, peel, quarter and slice the beetroot and put in a large bowl with the orange zest and juice, and the oil.
4 Add the rice, pistachios, feta cheese and mint. Season well. Mix in gently.
Per serving: Cals 338, Fat 14g, Sat Fat 5g, Carbs 40g

Beetroot, butternut and goats' cheese tartlets

This recipe can be used to make 6 individual tarts or 1 large one.

Serves 6 • Ready in 1 hr 40 mins

* 4 beetroot, peeled and cut into sixths
* 1 butternut squash, peeled and cut into chunks
* 2 red onions, peeled and cut into sixths
* Olive oil, for roasting
* Few sprigs rosemary
* 375 g | 13.2 oz pack ready-rolled all-butter shortcrust pastry
* 185 g | 6.5 oz crème fraîche
* 200 g | 7 oz goats' cheese, sliced into 6

YOU WILL NEED
* 6x7.5cm fluted loose-based flan tins, or a 20-23cm tin, baking parchment and baking beans

1 Heat the oven to 200°C/400°F/ Gas Mark 6. Place the vegetables in a roasting tin, toss with the oil and add the rosemary. Season well. Cook for around 30 mins, until the veg are soft and caramelised.
2 Meanwhile, use the pastry to line the tart tins, leaving an overhang. Place the tart tins on a baking sheet, line with baking parchment and fill with baking beans. Bake for 10-12 mins, then remove the baking beans and parchment and return to the oven for 5 mins, until the pastry is golden and cooked through. Remove from the oven and trim any overhanging pastry with a knife to form a neat edge.
3 Turn the oven down to 180°C/ 350°F/Gas Mark 4. Remove the parchment and baking beans and fill the tart cases with the roasted vegetables. Top each tart with 2tbsp crème fraîche and a slice of goats' cheese, then season again. Return to the oven and bake for 10-15 mins, until the cheese starts to become golden and bubbly. Serve with a salad of bitter leaves and tomatoes.
Per serving: Cals 609, Fat 44g, Sat Fat 20g, Carbs 42g

Twice-baked cheese soufflé

Prepare in advance and finish on the big day; a great way to get ahead this Christmas!

Serves 2 • Ready in 1 hr

* **175 ml | 5.9 fl oz milk**
* **1 shallot, halved**
* **½tsp pink peppercorns**
* **30 g | 1 oz unsalted butter, plus extra for greasing**
* **30 g | 1 oz plain flour**
* **½tsp Dijon mustard**
* **125 g | 4.4 oz Gruyère cheese, grated**
* **2 medium eggs, separated**
* **150 ml | 5 fl oz whipping cream**
* **60 g | 2 oz watercress, optional, to serve**

1 Preheat the oven to 200°C/400°F/Gas Mark 6. Heat the milk with the shallot and peppercorns, but don't boil. Grease the inside of 2 large ramekins.

2 Melt the butter in a pan, add the flour and stir to create a roux. Sieve milk mixture, removing the shallot and peppercorns and gradually whisk this into the roux to make a thick white sauce. Beat in the mustard, 100g cheese and the egg yolks, then season.

3 Whisk the egg whites until stiff, then fold in a spoonful to the cheese sauce to loosen, then fold in the remaining whites. Divide mixture between the ramekins and place in a large roasting tin filled with an inch of hot water. Bake for 20 mins, until well risen and beginning to colour.

4 Leave to cool; they will sink. Carefully loosen and turn soufflés out into individual heatproof dishes.

5 To serve, preheat the oven to 200°C/400°F/Gas Mark 6. Pour cream over each soufflé and sprinkle with the remaining cheese. Bake for 10-15 mins until golden and risen. Serve with watercress.

Per serving: Cals 866, Fat 73g, Sat Fat 44g, Carbs 20g

Mushroom and artichoke cups

Veggies don't have to miss out with this flavourful pate.

Serves 6 • Ready in 40 mins, plus cooling

* 100 g | 3.5 oz butter
* 150 g | 5.3 oz shallots, finely chopped
* 290 g | 10.2 oz jar marinated artichokes, drained and finely chopped
* 500 g | 17 oz chestnut mushrooms, roughly chopped
* 4 sprigs rosemary leaves, chopped (plus a few extra sprigs for the garnish)
* pinch grated whole nutmeg
* 4tbsp dry sherry
* 1tbsp sherry vinegar
* 200 g | 7 oz cream cheese

1 Heat half the butter in a large frying pan, add the shallots and fry until softened. Mix in the artichokes, turn up the heat and add the mushrooms, cooking for around 5 mins until they have reduced in size.

2 Add the rosemary and nutmeg and season. Add the sherry and vinegar and reduce by bubbling for a couple of mins. Remove from the heat and allow to cool.

3 Blend in the cream cheese, then spoon the mixture into espresso cups or small ramekins. Melt the rest of the butter and add a spoonful to each cup. Sprinkle with the rosemary, chill, then serve.

Per serving: Cals 360, Fat 36g, Sat Fat 19g, Carbs 4g

TIP
Swap artichokes for chestnuts for a delicious nutty flavour.

Layered fish cocktail

This tasty starter includes a delicious pea purée.

Serves 6 • Ready in 25 mins

- ✳ **300 g | 10.5 oz frozen petits pois**
- ✳ **100 ml | 3.5 fl oz milk**
- ✳ **2 tbsp fresh mint**
- ✳ **zest and juice of 1 lemon, plus lemon wedges, to serve**
- ✳ **125 g | 4.4 oz mayonnaise**
- ✳ **250 g | 8.8 oz prawns**
- ✳ **150 g | 5.3 oz hot smoked salmon**
- ✳ **125 g | 4.4 oz smoked salmon pâté**
- ✳ **18 crayfish**
- ✳ **6 small slices of smoked salmon**

YOU WILL NEED
- ✳ **6 serving bowls or dishes**

1 To make the pea purée, put the peas and milk in a saucepan and cook until just soft. Whizz up with the mint and lemon zest. Set aside to cool completely. Add the lemon juice to the mayonnaise and season with lots of black pepper.

2 Layer up in individual serving dishes, starting with the prawns, then the mayo, the hot smoked salmon, the pea purée, the pâté and the crayfish. Top with a slice of smoked salmon and serve with a wedge of lemon.

Per serving: Cals 317, Fat 22g, Sat fat 3g, Carbs 7g

Grilled goats' cheese and thyme toasts

Keep portions small as it's quite rich.

Serves 4 • Ready in 10 mins

✳ 1 small baguette, cut into 4
✳ 2 tbsp olive oil
✳ 4 tbsp fruity chutney
✳ 4 thick slices of soft goats' cheese (make sure you use a vegetarian variety if serving strict veggies)
✳ 1 small bunch of thyme, leaves removed
✳ salad leaves, to serve

1 Heat the grill. Put the baguette slices on a baking tray and drizzle over the oil. Grill for a few mins until crispy.
2 Remove from the oven and spread 1tbsp chutney on each piece of toasted baguette, then top with goats' cheese and sprinkle with thyme leaves. Grill for a further 5-8 mins until just toasted and softened. Serve with the salad.
Per serving: Cals 291, Fat 13g, Sat fat 5g, Carbs 32g

The Main EVENT

Turkey with pear and sausage stuffing

Succulent, moist and infused with flavour – bring to the table to carve.

Serves 6 • Ready in 3hrs 30 mins, plus resting

* 3.5-4kg | 7.7-8.8 lb turkey
* 50 g | 1.7 oz butter, softened
* 150 ml | 5.3 fl oz white wine
* juice of ½ lemon
* 12 chipolatas
* fresh herbs, to garnish

FOR THE STUFFING

* 50 g | 1.7 oz butter, softened
* 2 onions, chopped
* 3 sausages, skins removed and meat chopped
* 2 garlic cloves, crushed
* 2 pears, roughly chopped
* 200 ml | 7 fl oz chicken stock
* 200 g | 7 oz breadcrumbs
* 1 tbsp chopped fresh sage

1 Heat the oven to 180°C/350°F/Gas Mark 4. For the stuffing, melt the butter and cook the onions for 10 mins until soft. Then add the sausage meat, garlic and pears, and cook for 3 mins. Pour in the stock, bring to the boil and simmer for 2 mins. Stir in the breadcrumbs and sage, and season.

2 Spoon a third of the stuffing into the turkey neck, then secure with a skewer. Put the remaining stuffing in a greased baking dish.

3 Rub the turkey with butter, season and put it in a roasting tin, breast-side down. Pour the wine, lemon juice and 150ml water over the bird and roast for 2hrs, basting occasionally.

4 Turn the turkey over and cook for 30 mins or until the juices run clear. Transfer the turkey to a serving dish, wrap in foil and leave to rest. Increase the oven to 200°C/400°F/Gas Mark 6 and cook the chipolatas and separate stuffing for 30 mins.

5 Pour the juices from the roasting tin into a jug to make the gravy. Garnish the bird with herbs just before serving.

Per serving: Cals 750, Fat 37g, Sat fat 36g, Carbs 36g

TIP
Make the stuffing the day before, allow it to cool, then stuff the turkey on Christmas morning

Thyme and Prosecco parsnips

Prosecco makes a delicious glaze for parsnips.

Serves 6-8 · Ready in 40 mins

* **1kg | 2.2 lb parsnips, peeled and halved**
* **2tbsp olive oil**
* **250 ml | 8.8 fl oz Prosecco**
* **3-4 sprigs thyme**
* **25 g | 0.8 oz butter**

1 Heat the oven to 200°C/400°F/ Gas Mark 6. Toss the parsnips in the oil. Tip into a roasting tin and cook for 25 mins.

2 Meanwhile, bubble the Prosecco in a pan until reduced by half then add the thyme and butter for 2 mins. Pour over the parsnips and return to the oven for a further 10 mins.
Per serving: Cals 227-171, Fat 9-7g, Sat fat 3-2.5g, Carbs 21-16.5g

Glazed carrots

Balsamic red cabbage

Brussels sprouts with chestnuts

Roast potatoes

The fat you use is up to you, but for the crispiest results, always add a hot potato to hot fat.

Serves 6-8 • Ready in 1hr 30 mins

✳ **1.5kg | 3.3 lb King Edward potatoes, peeled and cut into chunks**
✳ **100 ml | 3.5 fl oz olive oil, goose fat or dripping**

1 Steam the potatoes until just tender, around 15-20 mins, or boil for 15 mins. Heat fat in a roasting tin until very hot. Drain and shake the potatoes to roughen up the edges.
2 Tip them into the hot roasting tin, coat with the fat and roast for 1hr-1hr 15mins at 200°C/400°F/ Gas Mark 6, basting midway. They should be lightly browned and crispy. Sprinkle with salt to serve.
Per serving: Cals 328-246, Fat 12.5g-9.5, Sat fat 2-1.5g, Carbs 47-35g

Glazed carrots

A roast dinner essential.

Serves 8 • Ready in 20 mins

✳ **500 g | 17 oz carrots, peeled and halved**
✳ **60 g | 2 oz butter**
✳ **1 Knorr Vegetable Stock Pot**
✳ **2 tbsp golden caster sugar**
✳ **400 ml | 14 fl oz orange juice**
✳ **2 tbsp chopped parsley**

Put everything together in a pan, bring to the boil, cover and cook for 5cmins. Uncover and simmer for 10 more mins, until the carrots are tender and the liquid turns to a syrupy glaze. Sprinkle with chopped parsley.
Per serving: Cals 114, Fat 6.5g, Sat fat 4g, Carbs 12g

Balsamic red cabbage

Serve any leftovers cold the next day for a different take on coleslaw.

Serves 8 • Ready in 1hr

✳ **1 tbsp light olive oil**
✳ **30 g | 1 oz butter**
✳ **2 onions, peeled and sliced**
✳ **1 small red cabbage, shredded**
✳ **2 cooking apples, peeled and chopped**
✳ **pared rind and juice of 1 orange**
✳ **100 ml | 3.5 fl oz balsamic vinegar**
✳ **4tbsp caster sugar**
✳ **1 cinnamon stick, broken into 2-3 pieces**

1 Heat the oil and butter in a large frying pan, add the onions and cook for 5mins until soft. Add the cabbage, apples, orange rind and juice, vinegar, sugar and cinnamon.
2 Cover the pan and cook on a low heat for 45cmins-1hr, stirring occasionally. Season to taste with salt and pepper.
Per serving: Cals 144, Fat 5g, Sat fat 2g, Carbs 20g

Brussels sprouts with chestnuts

No soggy Brussels here – lightly fried, they will have a slight crunch.

Serves 8 • Ready in 20 mins

✳ **1kg | 2.2 lb Brussels sprouts, trimmed**
✳ **200 g | 7 oz pack whole cooked chestnuts, halved**
✳ **30 g | 1 oz butter**

Blanch the sprouts in boiling water for 3 mins, drain and plunge into cold water. Drain and cover. To serve, fry the chestnuts and sprouts in butter for a few mins, to warm through.
Per serving: Cals 140, Fat 5.5g, Sat fat 2.5g, Carbs 13.5g

DON'T FORGET...
Pigs in blankets

Makes 12

Cut 6 pancetta slices in half and wrap them around 12 mini cooking chorizo. Put on a baking tray and bake for 20 mins at 200°C/400°F/Gas Mark 6.
Per pig in blanket: Cals 100, Fat 8g, Sat fat 3g, Carbs 0.5g

Madeira wine turkey gravy

Serves 8

Put the turkey giblets, 1 carrot, 1 onion, 1 celery stick, 2 bay leaves and peppercorns in a pan with 900 ml | 32 fl oz cold water. Cover and simmer for 45 mins. Skim once. While the turkey is resting, pour off as much of the fat in the roasting tin as you can, leaving the dark brown juices. Heat the tin on the hob, whisk in 40 g | 1.4 oz plain flour, then add 150 ml | 5.3 fl oz Madeira wine and bubble for 1 min. Pour in the stock, bring to the boil, then add 2tbsp redcurrant jelly and simmer for 5 mins. Season, then pour through a sieve into a sauce boat. Keep warm until ready to serve.
Per serving: Cals 118, Fat 5g, Sat fat 0.8g, Carbs 10g

Bread sauce

Serves 8

Simmer 1 small onion, 2 cloves, 2 bay leaves, 6 black peppercorns and 300 ml | 10.5 fl oz milk for 5 mins. Leave for 10mins for the favours to infuse. Strain the milk into a clean pan. Add 100 g | 3.5 oz crustless white bread, cut into cubes, 25 g | 0.8 oz butter, 4tbsp crème fraîche, ¼tsp freshly grated nutmeg. Heat, stirring occasionally, until the sauce thickens. Season and add a pinch of nutmeg.
Per serving: Cals 90, Fat 6g, Sat fat 4g, Carbs 6g

Cranberry vodka sauce

Serves 8

Tip 250 g | 8.8 oz fresh or frozen cranberries into a pan with 100 g | 3.5 oz golden caster sugar, 4 crushed juniper berries and 2tbsp vodka. Bring to the boil then simmer for 5-8 mins, stirring occasionally, until the sauce has thickened. The sauce will keep in the fridge for 1 week. Warm through to serve.
Per serving: Cals 62, Fat 0g, Carbs 13.5g

TIP
Prepare ahead and freeze, then defrost the sauces on Christmas morning

Nut roast with melting middle

A perfect festive veggie main.

Serves 6 • Ready in 45 mins

* **100 g | 3.5 oz each pecan and Brazil nuts**
* **60 g | 2 oz almonds, blanched**
* **2 tbsp pumpkin seeds**
* **25 g | 0.8 oz unsalted butter**
* **3 small onions, finely chopped**
* **2 garlic cloves, chopped**
* **2 tsp soy sauce**
* **1 tsp sherry vinegar**
* **½ tsp English mustard powder**
* **3 tbsp flat-leaf parsley, chopped**
* **1tbsp thyme leaves**
* **3 large eggs, beaten**
* **150 g | 5.3 oz Red Leicester or other hard cheese (make sure it's vegetarian if serving strict veggies), half grated, half cut into 6 cubes**
* **400 g | 14 oz can cherry tomatoes, drained**

YOU WILL NEED

* **6 dariole moulds or small, deep ramekins, oiled and the bases and sides lined with baking parchment**

1 Gently dry-toast the nuts and pumpkin seeds until golden. Allow to cool then pulse in a processor until finely chopped (not a powder).

2 Melt the butter in a pan and sweat the onions and garlic for 5 mins. Heat the oven to 180°C/350°F/Gas Mark 4 or 200°C/400°F/Gas Mark 6. In a large bowl, combine the nut mix with the onions and the remaining ingredients (except the cheese cubes). Season and mix well.

3 Fill the darioles three-quarters full, put a cube of cheese in each centre and cover with the remaining mix. Bake for 25-30 mins, then turn out onto serving plates and carefully peel away the baking parchment.
Per serving: Cals 536, Fat 46g, Sat fat 13g, Carbs 8.5g

Succulent ham with crackling

A baked ham, finished with crispy crackling, is a Christmas essential.

Serves 12 with leftovers • Ready in 3hrs 30 mins, plus resting

* 1 boneless gammon, around 4 kg | 8.8 lb, the skin scored
* 3 whole star anise
* 10 black peppercorns
* 3 onions, peeled and halved
* 1tsp sea salt

1 Heat the oven to 170°C/325°F/Gas Mark 3. Double-line a large roasting tin with a large piece of foil, big enough to wrap up the ham in a "tent". Put the ham in the centre, with the spices and onions around it. Sprinkle the skin with the salt, scrunch the foil to seal then bake for 3 hrs. The internal temperature should read 60°C/140°F when measured with a digital thermometer.

2 Increase the oven to 230°C/450°F/Gas Mark 8. Cover any exposed bits of ham with foil so only the skin is left unwrapped. Return the ham to the oven for a further 20-25 mins, until the majority of the skin has crackled and is crisp.
3 When the crackling is done, remove the ham, take off the foil and leave to rest for 30 mins.
Per serving: Cals 206, Fat 11g, Sat fat 4g, Carbs 0g

TIP
You can bake the ham to step 1 up to 3 days ahead and leave it uncovered in the fridge until you're ready to complete the recipe

Leek and lime salmon en croute

Spend half an hour preparing this impressive main course, then store in the freezer and cook from frozen. Extra hollandaise can be served on the side.

Serves 8 • Ready in 1hr

* 2 salmon fillets, skinned from a whole salmon (around 800g-1kg | 1.8-2.2 lb)
* 750 g | 1.6 lb puff pastry
* 1tbsp olive oil
* 400 g | 14 oz leeks, sliced and washed
* 2 tbsp polenta or cornmeal
* finely grated zest and juice of 2 limes
* 3tbsp hollandaise sauce
* 1 egg, beaten

1 Heat the oven to 220°C/ 425°F/Gas Mark 7. Trim off the tail end of the salmon fillets. Cut off a quarter of the pastry and roll out on a floured board to a shape just larger than one fillet. Put the pastry on a baking tray and bake for 10 mins.
2 Flatten gently with a fish slice, then bake for another 5-10 mins until golden, then cool.
3 Heat the oil and pan-fry the leeks for 10 mins. Sprinkle the pastry base with polenta (to stop a soggy base), and put 1 fillet on top. Season the fish, sprinkle over half the lime zest and juice, then spread over the hollandaise and leeks. Sprinkle lime zest and juice on the other fillet and put on top of the leeks.

4 Roll out the remaining pastry on baking parchment and run a lattice cutter over the pastry and ease apart for a lattice effect. Otherwise, score with a sharp knife. Brush the edges with the beaten egg and lay over the salmon, eggy side down. Tuck the edges under the base. Either bake at 220°C/450°F/Gas Mark 7 for 20-25 mins, or cover and freeze.
5 If cooking from frozen, brush the salmon en croute with beaten egg and bake at 220°C/450°F/Gas Mark 7 for 30mins. Then cover with foil and cook for 30 mins more.
Per serving: Cals 619, Fat 40g, Sat fat 15g, Carbs 37g

A make-ahead main that's fab to pull from the freezer when unexpected guests come calling

Roast rib of beef with mustard and horseradish crust

This is such a treat and any leftovers give wonderful cold cuts on Boxing Day.

Serves 6 with leftovers • Ready in 2hrs 40 mins, plus resting

* 3kg | 6.6 lb fore rib of beef (3-bone), chined
* 3tbsp grated horseradish
* 5tbsp wholegrain mustard
* 3 red onions, halved for the gravy
* 500 ml | 17 fl oz strong beef stock
* 200 ml | 7 fl oz full-bodied red wine (Shiraz would be perfect)
* 2tsp cornflour

1 Heat the oven to 240°C/475°F/ Gas Mark 9. Weigh your beef to get a rough idea of the cooking time, though we suggest you invest in a meat thermometer for accuracy. It's a shame to overcook such an expensive piece of meat, and a meat thermometer is pretty essential for the turkey too. Allow 40 mins per kg for medium rare.

2 Put the beef in a roasting tin. Season all over. Mix the horseradish and mustard together and spread over the fat. Any left or extras are delicious served with the beef. Put the onions around the beef. Roast for 15 mins then turn the oven down to 190°C/375°F/Gas Mark 5 and cook for your calculated cooking time, in this case, around 2hrs 30 mins. It should measure around 58°C/136°F on your oven thermometer from the oven, then 61-65°C/142-149°F after resting. Remove from the oven and leave to rest, lightly covered with foil.

3 Make the gravy by bubbling up the stock and the wine with the roasted red onions and any juices from the beef. Once the alcohol has burned off, strain then add the cornflour mixed with a little cold water to thicken.

Per serving: Cals 588, Fat 24g, Sat fat 10g, Carbs 9g

Herb-rolled leg of lamb

This is the perfect recipe for a crowd of friends and family to enjoy.

Serves 6 • Ready in 2hrs 20 mins

* **2 kg | 4.4 lb butterflied, boneless leg of lamb (ask your butcher to do this for you)**
* **400 ml | 14 fl oz white wine**
* **400 ml | 14 fl oz lamb or beef stock**
  FOR THE STUFFING
* **100 g | 3.5 oz pine nuts, lightly toasted**
* **large bunch of mint, leaves picked**
* **zest and juice of 1 unwaxed lemon**
* **75 g | 2.6 oz black pitted olives**
* **2 garlic cloves, crushed**
* **1 tsp ground cinnamon**
* **5 tbsp olive oil**

1 Heat the oven to 220°C/425°F/ Gas Mark 7. For the stuffing, whizz the pine nuts, mint, lemon zest and juice, olives, garlic, cinnamon and 3 tbsp of the olive oil in a food processor to a coarse mixture.
2 Lay out the lamb, skin-side down, on a chopping board, and season with salt and pepper. Spread the paste evenly over the meat, leaving a 3cm border around the edge. Tightly roll up the meat and tie at 5cm intervals with kitchen string, so you have a long round of meat. Rub over the remaining olive oil and season again.
3 Put the joint into a roasting tin and roast for 30 mins. Turn down the oven to 180°C/200°F/Gas Mark 4, pour the wine into the roasting tin and roast for a further 1hr. Remove the lamb from the roasting tin and leave to rest for up to 30 mins, while you make the gravy.
4 Pour the juices and any bits of stuffing from the roasting tin into a pan, skimming off the fat. Add the stock and warm through on a medium heat, adding any extra juices from the joint. Cut of the string, ready to carve.
Per serving: Cals 776, Fat 49g, Sat fat 14g, Carbs 2g

Pork roulade with parsnip and chestnut stuffing

This fancy roll is ideal for a Sunday roast or special Christmas dinner and is super-tender and delicious.

Serves 6 • Ready in 1 hr 30 mins, plus resting

- ✳ **2 x 550 g | 19.4 oz pork tenderloins or fillet**
- ✳ **100 g | 3.5 oz prosciutto**

FOR THE STUFFING
- ✳ **1 tbsp unsalted butter**
- ✳ **1 small onion, finely diced**
- ✳ **3 garlic cloves, peeled and crushed**
- ✳ **2 parsnips, finely chopped**
- ✳ **100 g | 3.5 oz cooked chestnuts, chopped**
- ✳ **1 tbsp sage, finely chopped**
- ✳ **2 tbsp apple juice**
- ✳ **30 g | 1 oz fresh white breadcrumbs**

FOR THE SAUCE
- ✳ **2 shallots, finely diced**
- ✳ **1 tbsp unsalted butter**
- ✳ **1 tsp cornflour, optional**
- ✳ **100 ml | 3.5 fl oz Rioja**
- ✳ **½ chicken stock cube**

1 Heat the oven to 200°C/400°F/ Gas Mark 6. For the stuffing, melt the butter in a pan. Add the onion, garlic and parsnips, and season. Cook over a low heat for 20-25 mins, stirring every 5 mins. Add the chestnuts, sage, apple juice and 1tsp sea salt. Cook for 15 mins more with the lid on, then mix together or whizz in a food processor. Mix in the breadcrumbs.

2 Butterfly both tenderloins (cut so they open like a book) and bash with the back of a rolling pin until about 1cm thick.

3 Lay out the prosciutto on parchment. Place a piece of meat on top. Season with sea salt and spread over the stuffing. Put the second piece of meat on top and roll up tightly using the paper. Tie with twine.

4 Put the pork on a tray, covered with foil. Cook for 40 mins. Remove the foil; cook for 10 more mins. Rest for 15 mins in foil.

5 For the sauce, sweat the shallots in the butter. Mix in the cornflour and deglaze with the wine. Reduce the liquid by half, add 200ml | 7 fl oz water and stock, bring to a boil and mix well.

6 Cut off twine and carve the meat.
Per serving: 407 calories, 16g fat, 6g sat fat, 18g carbs

TIP
For succulent, tender meat, don't skimp on the resting time, it's worth the wait

TIP
If your turkey is a different size it needs to cook for 30 mins to start then 20 mins per kg (2.2 lb) plus 90 mins at the lower temperature

Clementine-glazed turkey

Our traditional showstopper main has a hint of festive citrus.

Serves 8 • Ready in 4 hrs

- ✳ **6 kg | 13.2 lb whole turkey**
- ✳ **150 g | 5.3 oz butter, sliced, plus extra for greasing**
- ✳ **10 clementines**
- ✳ **1 fresh bouquet garni (1 sprig rosemary, parsley, thyme and 1 bay leaf tied together with string)**
- ✳ **10 long shallots, trimmed**
- ✳ **4tbsp clear honey**
- ✳ **3tbsp olive oil**
- ✳ **4 sheets of gold leaf**

FOR THE STUFFING BALLS
- ✳ **300 g | 10.5 oz sausage meat**
- ✳ **80 g | 2.8 oz whole cranberries**
- ✳ **200 g | 7 oz breadcrumbs**
- ✳ **4 pickled onions, finely chopped**
- ✳ **1 egg**
- ✳ **1tbsp chopped flat-leaf parsley**

FOR THE GRAVY
- ✳ **50 g | 1.7 oz cornflour, plus extra for dusting**
- ✳ **50 ml | 1.7 fl oz port**
- ✳ **400 ml | 14 oz vegetable stock**
- ✳ **pigs in blankets, to serve**

1 Heat the oven to 200°C/400°F/Gas Mark 6. Put the turkey on a roasting tray with a rack and let it come to room temperature.

2 Cover the turkey with the butter slices, and season. Quarter 1 clementine and put it in the turkey cavity with the bouquet garni. Place the shallots underneath the rack and cover the turkey loosely with tinfoil. Roast for 30 mins, then turn the oven down to 180°C/350°F/Gas Mark 4 and roast for 3 hrs 30 mins, basting every 30 mins, and removing foil 1hr before end of cooking time.

3 To make the glaze, juice and zest 4 clementines in a bowl and mix in the honey and oil. Brush the glaze on the turkey 45 mins before the end of cooking and again 15 mins before the end. When the turkey is cooked, juices should run clear and a temperature gauge should read 74°C/165°F. Drain turkey juices into a jug and cover the turkey loosely with

tinfoil and allow to rest for 20 mins.

4 Combine all the stuffing ball ingredients. Shape the mixture into balls about the size of a golf ball. Place them on a butter-greased baking tray and put in the oven 10 mins before the end of turkey cooking time. Cook for 30 mins or until cooked through.

5 For the gravy, spoon the fat from the top of the turkey juices into a pan. Heat on the hob. Add the cornflour and cook for 1 min. Stir in the port and cook until it's reduced. Stir in the stock gradually. Bring to the boil, then simmer for 5 mins or until thickened.

6 Transfer the turkey to a serving platter or board. Dress with the remaining clementines, coating them with gold leaf and halving some. Surround turkey with the stuffing balls and pigs in blankets. Serve, along with the gravy and shallots.

Per serving: Cals 877, Fat 33g, Sat fat 14g, Carbs 54g

Super-easy cranberry and port sauce

This sauce has an authentic tart flavour that brings out the best taste from your turkey.

Makes 200 g • Ready in 20 mins, plus cooling

- ✳ **200 g | 7 oz frozen whole cranberries, defrosted**
- ✳ **3 tbsp caster sugar**
- ✳ **100 ml | 3.5 fl oz port**

1 Place the cranberries, sugar and port in a pan and simmer for 5 mins.
2 Bring to the boil then cook on a medium heat for 10-12 mins until thick.
3 Allow to cool before serving.
Per serving: Cals 45, Fat 0g, Sat fat 0g, Carbs 8g

Classic bread sauce

The quintessential condiment to make to enjoy with your Christmas Day meal.

Makes 200 g • Ready in 20 mins, plus cooling

- ✳ **500 ml | 17 fl oz whole milk**
- ✳ **60 ml | 2 fl oz single cream**
- ✳ **50 g | 1.7 oz butter**
- ✳ **1 garlic clove**
- ✳ **1 bay leaf**
- ✳ **100 g | 3.5 oz breadcrumbs**

1 Combine the milk, cream, butter and garlic in a pan and season and add the bay leaf. Simmer for 10 mins.
2 Remove the garlic and bay leaf, then stir in the breadcrumbs and simmer for 5 mins until thick and creamy.
3 Serve immediately or let stand and then reheat before serving.
Per serving: Cals 92, Fat 7g, Sat fat 4g, Carbs 4g

Get-ahead gravy

If you want to get as much prep done as possible before Christmas Day, this gravy can be made a day or two before and kept in the fridge.

Serves 6 • Ready in 30 mins

- ✳ **600 ml | 21 oz or 1 pouch turkey or chicken stock**
- ✳ **300 ml | 10.5 oz Amontillado sherry or Madeira wine**
- ✳ **2 tsp cornflour**
- ✳ **1 bay leaf**

1 Bubble the stock with the sherry or wine until the alcohol has burned off, then add the bay leaf.
2 Mix the cornflour with cold water and add this paste to the stock. Bubble until thickened.
3 Remove the bay leaf. Reheat when you're ready to serve, adding butter and seasoning well. And some chefs swear by adding a squashed roast potato to their gravy just before serving.
Per serving: Cals 90, Fat 4.2g, Sat fat 1.8g, Carbs 1.2g

Chicken and apricot pâté with toast thins

TIP
Short on time?
Peter's Yard
sourdough
crispbreads are to
accompany the
pâté

Chicken and apricot pâté with toast thins

A rich and sticky pâté that gets a festive makeover.

Serves 8 • Ready in 1 hr 40 mins, plus chilling time

* **250 g | 8.7 oz apricots or 200g | 7 oz hydrated dried apricots, de-stoned and finely chopped**
* **1 tbsp clear honey**
* **1 tbsp white wine vinegar**
* **200g | 7 oz butter**
* **2 garlic cloves, crushed**
* **6 shallots, finely chopped**
* **1 tsp grated fresh nutmeg**
* **1 tsp ground cinnamon**
* **100ml | 3.5 fl oz sherry**
* **700g | 25 oz chicken livers**
* **4 eggs**
* **Bunch fresh coriander, chopped, plus extra sprigs, for garnish**
* **8 slices of white bread**
* **edible gold spray (optional)**

YOU WILL ALSO NEED
* **1kg loaf tin, greased and lined with parchment paper**

1 Heat the oven to 140°C/275°F/Gas Mark 1.
2 In a small pan, cover the apricots with 100ml boiling water and add the honey and vinegar. Bring to the boil then simmer for 10-12 mins, until it turns into a thick compote. Let it cool.
3 Spread half of the apricot compote evenly into the base of the lined tin.
4 Melt 20g of the butter in a pan and fry the garlic and shallots for 5 mins, then add the nutmeg, cinnamon and sherry. Reduce until the sherry has evaporated.
5 In a food processor, blend the onion mix together with the livers. Add the eggs and combine well.
Melt the remaining butter then pour into the liver mix and blend again until incorporated. Pass the mixture through a sieve into a jug then season with sea salt and coarsely ground pepper. Stir in the coriander.
6 Fill the tin with the liver mixture, then wrap with a double sheet of tinfoil, making sure it is completely covered. Place the tin in a roasting tin half filled with boiling water and put in the oven. Cook for 1 hr until an inserted skewer comes out hot. Let it cool completely, then chill for 4 hrs.
7 Toast the bread, then trim the crusts and discard. Half vertically, in between the 2 toasted sides by laying the toast flat on a chopping board and slicing in between with a bread knife so you have 2 very thin pieces of bread. Heat the grill and grill the untoasted sides of the toast for 1-2 mins until golden. Cut each piece in half and then halve again to make small triangles.
8 Turn the pate onto a large plate and remove the parchment paper. Put the remaining apricot on top and garnish with coriander sprigs and spray the apricot topping with the edible gold spray, if using. Surround with the toast thins and serve.
Per serving: Cals 504, Fat 35g, Sat fat 17g, Carbs 28g

Trio of green, white and red cabbage

This simple side complements a rich meal perfectly.

Serves 8 • Ready in 20 mins

* **1 small Savoy cabbage**
* **½ red cabbage**
* **½ white cabbage**
* **1 tbsp butter**

Shred each cabbage thinly then place the Savoy and white cabbage in a large pan and the red cabbage in a separate pan. Fill both pans with boiling water until the cabbage is covered, then simmer for 10 mins. Drain and combine in a serving bowl. Add the butter and season with lots of black pepper. Toss together and serve.
Per serving: Cals 63, Fat 2g, Sat fat 1g, Carbs 1g

**Mushroom
and Brie
cracker**

Mushroom and Brie cracker

A fun, tasty veggie option.

Serves 6-8 • Ready in 1 hr 5 mins

- 200 g | 7 oz frozen whole cranberries, defrosted, keeping some for garnish
- 1 tbsp caster sugar
- 750 g | 26 oz chestnut mushrooms
- 100 g | 3.5 oz unsalted butter
- 4 garlic cloves, crushed
- 1 onion, chopped
- 2 tbsp dry sherry
- 200 g | 7 oz breadcrumbs
- 30 g | 1 oz chopped chives, reserving
- 8 whole chives for garnish
- 200 g | 7 oz Brie
- 12 sheets filo pastry

1 Place the cranberries in a pan and add the sugar and 150 ml cold water. Season with pepper and bring to the boil. Simmer for 12-15 mins until it's a thick and glossy sauce. Let it cool.
2 Chop half of the mushrooms into quarters then halve again. Blend the rest until they're a paste-like consistency. Strain off excess liquid.
3 Melt 20 g of the butter in a large pan and add the garlic and onion. Sauté for 8 mins, until softened, then add the quartered mushrooms and fry, stirring occasionally for 4 mins. Add the sherry and reduce down until it's evaporated. Mix in the blended mushrooms, breadcrumbs and chives, and season. Let it cool.
4 Heat the oven to 200C°C/400°F/ Gas Mark 6. Slice the Brie into strips around 3cm thick and set aside. Melt the remaining butter in the microwave until it's a liquid and grease a large flat baking tray.
5 Lay out a sheet of baking paper and put 10 of the filo pastry sheets on it. Brush the filo together with the melted butter and layer to make a piece of pastry measuring 30 x 30cm. Allowing a 7cm border, apart from the longer side you start from, spread the cranberry sauce in a rectangle and top with the mushroom mixture. Line up the Brie in a single row horizontally down the middle of the mushrooms, then roll the pastry around it to make a sausage shape. Twist the ends to create a cracker shape. Transfer to the prepared tray using the baking paper. Brush 1 of the leftover filo pastry sheets with butter, fold in half lengthways and wrap around one of the cracker's ends. Do the same with the other end. Brush the whole cracker with melted butter. Bake for 15-20 mins. Slice the reserved chives in 2 lengthways, put in cold water, to curl. Decorate cracker ends with them and the reserved whole cranberries.
Per serving: Cals 478-638, Fat 19-25g, Sat fat 11-15g, Carbs 65-86g

Parmesan mashed potato

A cheesy alternative to roasties.

Serves 8 • Ready in 20 mins

- 1kg | 2.2 lb Maris Piper potatoes, chopped
- 45 g | 1.5 oz grated Parmesan, plus shavings for garnish
- 1 tbsp unsalted butter
- 2 tbsp crème fraiche
- 2 tbsp chopped flat-leaf parsley, plus leaves for garnish

1 Bring the potatoes to the boil. Simmer for 12-15 mins until soft. Drain then mash with the Parmesan, butter and crème fraiche. Season with pepper and mix in the parsley.
2 Transfer to a serving bowl. Top with Parmesan shavings and parsley.
Per serving: Cals 149, Fat 5g, Sat fat 3g, Carbs 23g

TIP Serve, just after adding the butter, for the full effect before it melts

Sprouts with chestnut and fig butter

Take the sprouts to the next level with this luxurious butter.

Serves 8 • Ready in 20 mins, plus chilling

- 80 g | 3 oz butter, softened
- 50 g | 1.7 oz soft figs
- 100 g | 3.5 oz cooked chestnuts
- 1 tbsp finely chopped parsley
- 800 g | 28 oz Brussels sprouts, trimmed

1 In a food processor, combine the butter, figs and half the chestnuts. Season with pepper and blend until smooth and combine. Mix in the parsley and crumble in the remaining chestnuts. Stir briefly then transfer to a large piece of baking paper. Roll the butter into a sausage shape using the paper then wrap it around the butter and twist the ends so it's like a cracker. Chill for 1 hr.
2 Put the sprouts in a large pan and cover with boiling water. Simmer for 5-8 mins. Transfer them to a serving bowl, then slice the butter and scatter it on top.
Per serving: Cals 162, Fat 10g, Sat fat 5g, Carbs 17g

Roast sweet potatoes and garlic with thyme

The perfect combination, these will be popular on Christmas Day.

Serves 8 • Ready in 1 hr

* rapeseed oil, for roasting
* 1 kg | 2.2 lb sweet potatoes, peeled
* 2 garlic heads, halved horizontally
* 6 sprigs fresh thyme

1 Heat the oven to 200°C/400°F/Gas Mark 6. Fill a roasting tray a third of the way up with oil and place in the oven.
2 Chop each sweet potato into 3 or 4 pieces, depending on its size then transfer to a large pan. Cover the sweet potatoes with cold water and bring to the boil. Simmer for 5 mins and drain thoroughly.
3 With tongs, carefully transfer the sweet potatoes to the hot oil. Cook for 40-45 mins until golden, adding the garlic 30 mins before the end of cooking and turning the potatoes every 15 mins or so.
4 Transfer potatoes to a serving bowl. Add the garlic. Season with sea salt, black pepper. Garnish with thyme.
Per serving: Cals 222, Fat 12g, Sat fat 1g, Carbs 28g

TIP
Using lots of oil will crisp up these beauties

TIP
Make the nuts ahead of time. You can also make extra to snack on or give as edible gifts

Vegan root vegetable wreath with garlic and dill sauce

This mouthwatering wreath uses shop-bought vegan puff pastry making it an easy festive main everyone can enjoy!

Serves 6 • Ready in 1 hr 30 mins, plus chilling

- Plain flour for dusting
- 500 g | 17 oz block Jus-Rol vegan pastry
- 4tbsp olive oil, plus extra for frying and roasting
- 3tbsp maple syrup
- 2 garlic cloves, crushed
- 3tbsp fresh thyme leaves, finely chopped
- 500 g | 17 oz heritage carrots, peeled and cut into 1cm thick rounds
- 200 g | 7 oz parsnips, peeled, topped and cut into 1cm thick rounds
- 1 large red onion, thinly sliced into half moons
- 1tbsp mustard seeds
- 1tbsp oat milk or milk alternative (we used Oatly Oat drink)
- 20 g | 0.7 oz sugar
- 1tsp nutmeg
- 50 g | 1.7 oz hazelnuts

FOR THE SAUCE
- 1 bulb of garlic
- bunch dill, fronds stripped from the stem
- 200 g | 7 oz vegan crème fraiche alternative (we used Oatly Creamy Oat Fraiche)

YOU WILL NEED
- A small bowl approximately 16cm in diameter

1 Flour your work surface and roll out your pastry to 30cm x 30cm square. Cut out a large circle and then transfer to a lined baking tray. Place your small bowl in the centre of the pastry circle and lightly press it down, ensuring you don't go all the way through. Remove the bowl and cut the inner circle into 8 triangles. Cut alternating triangles in half, lengthways. Chill in the fridge for 30 mins.

2 Heat the oven to 200°C/400°F/ Gas Mark 6. In a large bowl, mix 2tbsp oil with 2tbsp maple syrup, garlic and 2tbsp thyme leaves. Add the carrots and parsnips and mix to ensure they are fully coated. Season with salt and pepper and spread over a baking tray in a single layer. Cook in the oven for 20-25 mins, until just soft. Slice the bottom of the bulb of garlic, drizzle over 1tbsp olive oil, wrap in foil and cook in the oven for 20 minutes until soft.

3 Meanwhile, heat 1tbsp olive oil in a frying pan and cook the onions until soft and translucent but not brown. Add the mustard seeds and cook for a further min and allow to cool.

4 To assemble, take your pastry from the fridge, spoon the onions around the edge then arrange the roasted carrots and parsnips on top. Take the four triangles and pull these over the veggies, securing the corners on the edge of the wreath. With the triangles previously cut in half, carefully twist these and pull over the veggies as stated previously.

5 Combine 1tbsp maple syrup with the oat milk and brush over the pastry to glaze. Cook for 25-30 mins until the pastry is nice and golden.

6 Meanwhile, dissolve the sugar in 20ml of water in a saucepan. Add the nutmeg, 1tbsp thyme leaves and the hazelnuts. Spoon onto a lined-baking sheet, season generously and cook for 15-20 mins until nicely brown and roasted. Allow to cool slightly and then roughly chop.

7 To make your garlic and dill dip, squeeze the soft, roasted garlic from its skin and roughly chop with the dill fronds. Mix with the creamy oat fraiche and season. When your wreath, is cooked transfer to a large plate, sprinkle over the chopped hazelnuts and serve with the dill and garlic sauce.
Per serving: Cals 617, Fat 40g, Sat Fat 14g, Carbs 52g

Fennel and orange salad with blue cheese

Don't underestimate this simple salad, it has a wonderful flavour and great crunch.

Serves 8 • Ready in 20 mins

- ✷ 2 fennel bulbs, tops removed and fronds reserved
- ✷ 50 g | 1.7 oz roasted almonds
- ✷ 3 oranges, segmented
- ✷ 150 g | 5.3 oz Stilton
- **FOR THE DRESSING**
- ✷ 4tbsp extra virgin olive oil
- ✷ 2tbsp white wine or sherry vinegar

1 Make the dressing by whisking the ingredients together and set aside.
2 Cut the fennel bulbs into quarters and remove the core. Using a mandolin or speed peeler, thinly slice the fennel, transfer to a large bowl and toss in the dressing. Add the nuts and the orange segments and toss carefully, trying not to break up the segments.
3 Pile the salad onto a large platter and crumble over the Stilton and garnish with the fennel fronds.
Per serving: Cals 172, Fat 15.5g, Sat Fat 5.5g, Carbs 51g

Charred hispi cabbage with miso

If you're going to make one new thing this year, make sure it's this, so delicious!

Serves 8 • Ready in 1 hr

- ✷ 2 hispi cabbages
- ✷ 4tbsp olive oil
- ✷ 150 g | 5.3 oz butter, softened
- ✷ 45 g | 1.5 oz organic gluten-free miso paste
- ✷ 2 cloves garlic
- **FOR THE DRESSING**
- ✷ 4tbsp tahini
- ✷ 1tbsp sesame oil
- ✷ 2tbsp water
- ✷ 1tbsp maple syrup
- ✷ 1tsp ginger, minced
- ✷ Sanchi Furikake, to garnish

1 Heat a griddle pan on high. Cut the cabbages in half, and then divide in half again, or thirds depending on the size. Remove as much of the hard core as you can but still keeping the wedges intact. Brush the cut sides with oil and place on the griddle pan and for around 8 mins before repeating on the other side. This will have to be done in batches. Transfer to a baking tray, charred side up until all of the wedges are charred.
2 Heat the over to 190°C/375°F/Gas Mark 5. Mix the butter, miso and garlic together and spread all over the charred cabbage, making sure to get into all of the nooks and crannies. Roast in the oven for 25 mins, basting halfway through. Once cooked, transfer to a serving platter.
3 To make the dressing, whisk all of the ingredients together and pour over the cabbage. Garnish with Sanchi Furikake seasoning if you have – if not, black and white sesame seeds are great.
Per serving: Cals 290, Fat 27g, Sat Fat 11.5g, Carbs 6g

Hasselback carrots with hazelnut crumble

A fun and elegant way to serve carrots, and the crumble adds great texture.

Serves 6 • Ready in 1 hr

* ✳ 750 g | 26 oz heritage carrots
* ✳ 2tbsp olive oil
* ✳ 1tbsp maple syrup
* ✳ 1tsp cumin seeds

FOR THE CRUMBLE

* ✳ 50g | 1.7 oz whole roasted hazelnuts
* ✳ 1tbsp hazelnut oil
* ✳ 1tsp maple syrup
* ✳ 1tbsp watercress
* ✳ Pinch of salt

1 Heat the oven to 200°C/400°F/Gas Mark 6. Peel the carrots – if any are particularly thick, cut these in half lengthwise. To create the hasselback effect, take a pair of chopsticks and place either side of the carrot. Using a sharp knife, make cuts 3-5mm apart down the length of the carrot – the chopsticks will prevent you slicing all the way through. Place in a baking tray and drizzle over the oil, maple syrup and cumin seeds. Roast in the over for 35-40 mins.

2 Meanwhile, make the crumble by adding all of the ingredients to a food processor and blitz to a crumble. Once the carrots have been removed from the oven, garnish with the crumble.
Per serving: Cals 155, Fat 10g, Sat Fat 1g, Carbs 12.5g

Cheesy, sage and truffle hasselback potatoes

These decadent potatoes are the ultimate side for your veggie Christmas.

Serves 6 • Ready in 1 hr

* ✳ 600 g | 21 oz new potatoes
* ✳ 2tbsp olive oil
* ✳ 25g | 0.8 oz butter, plus more for frying
* ✳ 10 sage leaves
* ✳ 40 g | 1.4 oz vegetarian Italian hard cheese, finely grated
* ✳ 1tbsp truffle oil

1 Heat the oven to 200°C/400°F/Gas Mark 6. Slice your potatoes into hasselbacks. The easiest way to do this is to place the potato between two chopsticks – this way your knife won't go all the way through. Make the slices approx 3-5mm apart.

2 Put the olive oil and butter on a baking tray and place in the oven until melted and hot. Remove from the oven and carefully place your potatoes, sliced side facing up. Baste in the oil, season generously with salt and pepper and cook for 25 mins.

3 Meanwhile, melt some more butter in a frying pan and fry the sage leaves until crispy. Drain on some kitchen towel, until ready to serve.

4 Baste the potatoes again and sprinkle over half the cheese. Cook for another 25 mins until soft in the middle and crisp on the top.

5 Once the potatoes are cooked, drizzle over the truffle oil and remaining cheese. Spoon into a serving dish and scatter over the crispy sage leaves.
Per serving: Cals 188, Fat 11.5g, Sat Fat 4.5g, Carbs 15.5g

TIP
To make these vegan, swap the butter for 2 additional tbsp olive oil and omit the Italian hard cheese or use a vegan alternative

Beetroot and celeriac remoulade

Celeriac can often be overlooked, but this way of preparing it is super delicious.

Serves 6 • Ready in 15 mins

- 1 small celeriac
- 3 beetroot
- 1 small eating apple
- 150 ml | 5.3 fl oz crème fraîche
- 4tbsp mayonnaise
- 3tbsp extra virgin olive oil
- 2tsp Dijon mustard
- Juice of a lemon
- Salt and freshly ground black pepper
- Handful of roughly chopped flat-leaf parsley

1 Peel then coarsely grate or julienne the celeriac, beetroot and apple. Tip into a large bowl.

2 In a small bowl, mix the crème fraîche, mayonnaise, oil, mustard and lemon juice. Season well then stir into the beetroot mixture, until everything is just coated. Add the parsley and gently mix.

Per serving: Cals 272, Fat 24g, Sat Fat 8g, Carbs 8g

Braised chard with chilli and garlic

This is a great way of cooking robust greens such as chard, kale or cavolo nero.

Serves 6 • Ready in 20 mins

- ✳ 2tbsp olive oil, plus extra to serve
- ✳ 2 garlic cloves, chopped
- ✳ ½tsp chilli flakes
- ✳ 1 kg | 2.2 lb rainbow chard
- ✳ Juice of ½ lemon

1 Heat the oil in a large, heavy-based pan over a medium heat. Add the garlic and chilli flakes and cook for 1 min. Add the chard. Season with salt and pour in 200ml water.
2 Bring to the boil and cover. Cook for at least 10-15 mins, or until very tender and all the water has been absorbed, adding more water and cooking for longer if needed. Squeeze the lemon juice over the top and serve with a drizzle of olive oil.
Per serving: Cals 66, Fat 4g, Sat Fat 0.5g, Carbs 5g

Roasted pumpkin with a walnut, orange and parsley dressing

A great dish, and one that can be prepared ahead of time if you prefer to serve it as a salad at room temperature.

Serves 6 • Ready in 30 mins

- ✳ **1 medium pumpkin or squash, about 1.25-1.5 kg | 2.7-3.3 lb**
- ✳ **2tbsp olive oil**
FOR THE DRESSING
- ✳ **50 g | 1.7 oz walnuts, chopped**
- ✳ **Generous handful flat-leaf parsley, chopped**
- ✳ **1 garlic clove, finely chopped**
- ✳ **A good pinch of chilli flakes**
- ✳ **100 ml | 3.5 fl oz olive oil**
- ✳ **Juice and grated zest of 1 large orange**

1 Combine all the dressing ingredients and season with salt to taste. Set aside. Preheat the oven grill to medium-high, or heat your barbecue or fire pit until the flames have died down and the coals or wood have started to turn to ash.
2 Wash the pumpkin or squash, then cut in half and scoop out the seeds. don't peel. Cut into 1.5cm slices.
3 Toss the slices into a bowl with the olive oil and season. If cooking outdoors, lay the slices directly onto the barbecue grill and cook, turning every 2 mins, until charred and cooked through. If cooking indoors, place the slices on a baking sheet and grill until charred on both sides and tender.
4 To serve, arrange the slices on a platter and spoon over some of the dressing. Serve the remaining dressing on the side.
Per serving: Cals 284, Fat 22g, Sat Fat 3g, Carbs 16g

Bakes & DESSERTS

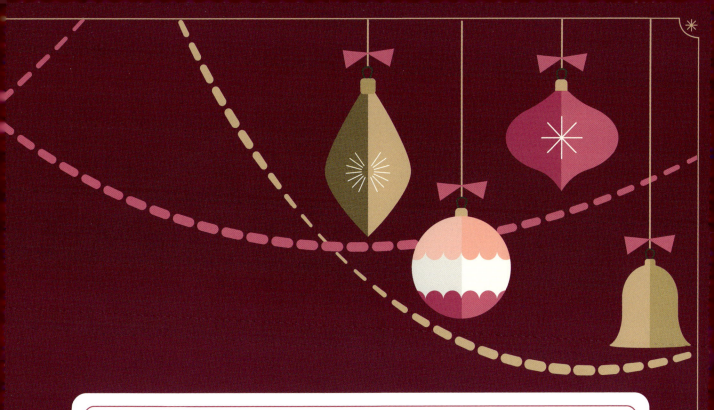

Bakewell mince pies

Add a little twist to your mince pies and top them with frangipane.

Makes 22-24 • Ready in 1 hr 30 mins

* **90 g | 3 oz butter, softened**
* **90 g | 3 oz caster sugar**
* **90 g | 3 oz ground almonds**
* **30 g | 1 oz plain flour**
* **1 large egg, beaten**
* **400 g | 14 oz block shortcrust pastry**
* **400 g | 14 oz jar good vegetarian mincemeat**
* **1 apple, grated**
* **A few flaked almonds, optional**
* **Icing sugar, for dusting**

1 Beat the butter and sugar until soft. Stir in the ground almonds, flour and egg, then set aside.
2 Roll out the pastry to the thickness of a £1 coin, and then cut out rounds to line 2 12-hole shallow bun tins. Collect the trimmings and re-roll – continue until all the pastry has been used. Leave to chill while the oven heats up to 180°C/350°F/Gas Mark 4.
3 Mix the grated apple and mincemeat together and spoon 1tbsp into each pastry case. Top with 2tsp of the almond topping and then sprinkle with flaked almonds.
4 Bake for 35 mins until golden, switching the trays around in the oven halfway through. Cool in the tray for 5 mins, then put the pies onto a wire rack and leave them to cool. Dust with icing sugar before serving.
Per serving: Cals 220, Fat 12.5g, Sat Fat 4.5g, Carbs 23g

Easy gluten-free mince pies

Shop-bought pastry means these mince pies can be made in no time at all!

Makes 12 • Ready in 25 mins

* **400 g | 14 oz gluten-free shortcrust pastry (we recommend Genius)**
* **1 jar vegetarian mincemeat**
* **1 egg, beaten**

YOU WILL NEED
* **2 x 12 hole muffin tray**
* **10cm round cutter**
* **Star cutter**

1 Heat the oven to 200°C/400°F/ Gas Mark 6. Roll out the shortcrust pastry to the thickness of a £1 coin and cut out 18 circles; 12 for the bases and the rest to top the pies.
2 Line the muffin tray with the pastry discs and divide the mincemeat evenly.
3 Using the star cutter, cut 6 stars from the centre of the remaining pastry discs. Add the starts to 6 of the pies, and the disc with the cut outs to the rest; securing the edges with a little beaten egg. Brush the tops of the pastry with egg and bake for 12-15 mins, until lightly browned and your house smells like Christmas!
Per serving: Cals 255, Fat 12g, Sat Fat 4g, Carbs 32g

Vegan cranberry mince pie pockets

Compromise nothing with these light and flaky vegan festive pastries.

Makes 24 • Ready in 30 mins

* **2 packets ready-rolled vegan puff pastry (we used Jus-Rol)**
* **320 g | 11 oz jar organic vegetarian mincemeat (we recommend Meridian)**
* **200 g | 7 oz cranberry sauce**
* **2tbsp dairy-free milk, such as oat milk or soya**

1 Heat the oven to 200°C/400°F/ Gas Mark 6. Mix the mincemeat with the cranberry sauce and set aside. Unravel the pastry, one at a time and cut each one into 12 squares.
2 Divide the mincemeat, placing a dollop in the centre of each square. Lightly brush the edges with dairy-free milk. Take the top left corner and pull over to the bottom right to create triangles, crimp the edges with a fork to bind the pastry.
3 Transfer to two lined baking trays and brush the tops with dairy-free milk. Using a pair of scissors, snip a little hole in the top of each pie to allow the steam to escape. Bake for 20 mins until puffed and golden. Cool slightly before serving.
Per serving: Cals 150, Fat 7g, Sat Fat 3g, Carbs 20g

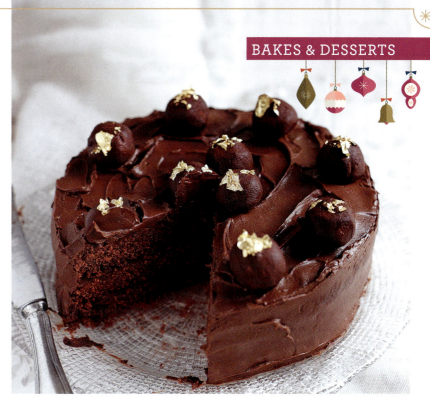

Spiced tree-shaped biscuits

The addition of ground spices to the dusting of icing sugar makes all the difference to these festive favourites

**Makes 25, depending on size •
Ready in 20 mins, plus chilling**

- ✳ **225 g | 7.8 oz unsalted butter, softened**
- ✳ **150 g | 5.3 oz icing sugar, plus extra for dusting**
- ✳ **1 large egg, beaten**
- ✳ **Grated zest of ½ unwaxed lemon**
- ✳ **350 g | 12 oz plain flour, plus extra for dusting**
- ✳ **¼tsp freshly ground nutmeg**
- ✳ **½tsp mixed spice**
- ✳ **Pinch of salt**

FOR DUSTING
- ✳ **100 g | 3.5 oz icing sugar**
- ✳ **1tsp ground cinnamon (ideally freshly ground)**
- ✳ **½tsp freshly ground nutmeg**

1 Beat together the softened butter and icing sugar in a large bowl, until light and fluffy. Gradually add the beaten egg, mixing well until smooth. Add the lemon zest and mix again.
2 Sift the plain flour, nutmeg, mixed spice and a pinch of salt into the bowl and mix until smooth. Shape the mixture into a disc, wrap in cling film and chill until firm. Line 2 baking sheets with greaseproof paper and set aside.
3 Lightly dust the worksurface with plain flour and roll the dough out to a thickness of 3mm. Using tree-shaped cutters stamp out biscuits and arrange on the prepared baking sheets. The number of biscuits you can make will depend on the size of your cutters. Chill for 20 mins and preheat the oven to 180°C/350°F/ Gas Mark 4.
4 Bake the biscuits in the oven for 10-12 mins or until pale golden. Once cooled, dust with icing sugar spiced with cinnamon and nutmeg.
Per serving: Cals 162, Fat 8g, Sat Fat 5g, Carbs 21g

Chocolate truffle cake

A rich vegan and gluten-free chocolate cake all can enjoy!

Serves 12 • Ready in 1 hr 15 mins, plus chilling

- ✳ **325 g | 11 oz gluten-free plain flour**
- ✳ **6tbsp cocoa powder, plus extra for the truffles**
- ✳ **250 g | 8.8 oz caster sugar**
- ✳ **250 g | 8.8 oz light muscovado sugar**
- ✳ **2tbsp gluten-free baking powder**
- ✳ **2tbsp cider vinegar**
- ✳ **2tsp vanilla extract**
- ✳ **400 g | 14 oz tin coconut milk**
- ✳ **400 g | 14 oz good-quality vegan dark chocolate, broken into chunks**
- ✳ **3tbsp raspberry jam**
- ✳ **Edible gold leaf**

1 Preheat the oven to 180°C/ 350°F/ Gas Mark 4. Sift the flour and cocoa powder together in a bowl and stir in the sugars and baking powder.
2 Stir the vinegar and vanilla together with 500ml water. Then, slowly beat the wet mix into the flour to make a batter. Grease and line 3 x 20cm sponge tins with baking paper. Pour ⅓ of the batter into each tin and bake all three sponges for 25-30 mins, until firm but springy in the centre. Leave the cakes to cool in the tins.
3 To make the ganache, pour half the coconut milk in a pan and heat until almost boiling. Take off the heat and stir in the chocolate until melted. Stir in the rest of the coconut milk. Divide the ganache between 2 bowls and chill in the fridge. Leave one bowl for 8 hrs or overnight to set very firmly; remove the other bowl 2 hrs before needed, so it's at room temperature.
4 To assemble, spread the cakes thinly with a little jam and then a little of the softer ganache. Place the cake layers on top of each other and spread the remaining ganache over the top and sides with a palette knife.
5 To make the truffles, scoop up 1tsp of firm ganache at a time, drop it into some cocoa powder and roll into a ball. Repeat. Decorate the cake with the truffles and gold leaf, if using.
Per serving: Cals 531, Fat 17g, Sat Fat 11.5g, Carbs 86g

Plum, amaretti and mascarpone bake

Recent studies have shown that plums match 'superfood' blueberries in antioxidants.

Serves 6 • Ready in 50 mins

* 10 ripe, red-fleshed plums, halved and stoned
* 50 g | 1.7 oz caster sugar
* 1tsp cornflour
* 75 ml | 2.6 fl oz amaretto
* 2 amaretti biscuits, crushed
* 125 g | 4.4 oz reduced-fat mascarpone, beaten until smooth

YOU WILL NEED
* A 23cm baking dish

1 Heat the oven to 200°C/400°F/ Gas Mark 6. Arrange the halved plums cut-side up in the baking dish. Mix together the caster sugar and cornflour and scatter over the fruit, then drizzle with the amaretto.
2 Bake for 35 mins, or until the juices run and the fruit is fragrant and soft. Scatter over one crushed biscuit, spread the mascarpone in mounds all over the top, then sprinkle with the crumbs of the second crushed biscuit. Cook for a further 4 mins in the oven and serve hot.
Per serving: Cals 161, Fat 7g, Sat Fat 2g, Carbs 21g

Gluten-free chocolate biscuits

There's no added sugar in this recipe – chocolate adds all the sweetness you need.

Makes 15 • Ready in 30 mins, plus chilling

* 1 egg
* 50 g | 1.7 oz ground almonds
* 100 g | 3.5 oz Doves Farm gluten-free plain flour
* 2 tbsp double cream
* 75 g | 2.6 oz unsalted butter
* 1 tsp vanilla extract
* 75 g | 2.6 oz dark chocolate, melted, but cool
* 50 g | 1.7 oz chopped roasted hazelnuts
* 45 g | 1.4 oz desiccated coconut

1 Heat the oven to 180°C/350°F/ Gas Mark 4. Using an electric mixer, beat together the egg and almonds. Add the flour, cream, butter, vanilla extract and chocolate, and beat until combined. Chill for 15 mins.
2 Remove from the fridge and roll the mixture into 15 balls. Roll each ball in the coconut and hazelnuts, and chill until firm, around 10 mins.
3 Bake on a baking tray for 10-12 mins, until the coconut is golden.
Per biscuit: Cals 166, Fat 13g, Sat fat 6g, Carbs 9g

Irish coffee meringue roulade

This boozy gluten-free roulade will cure any sweet tooth!

Serves 12 · Ready in 1 hr 30 mins

* 4 large egg whites
* 125 g | 4.4 oz golden caster sugar
* 2tsp gluten-free cornflour
* 300 ml | 10.5 fl oz double cream
* 3tbsp cocoa powder
* 2tbsp whisky
* 2tbsp Bailey's liqueur
* 1tbsp icing sugar
* 50 g | 1.7 oz chocolate-covered coffee beans
* 100 g | 3.5 oz gluten-free dark chocolate
* 2tbsp double cream

1 Heat oven to 150°C/300°F/Gas Mark 2. Line a 30 x 20cm Swiss roll tin with baking paper.
2 Whisk the egg whites until stiff, then add the sugar until the mix is stiff. Whisk in the cornflour. Spread the meringue evenly in the tin and bake for 1 hr. Leave to cool in the tin.
3 Whisk the cream, 2tbsp cocoa, whisky and Bailey's together to form soft peaks. Sieve the remaining cocoa and icing sugar over a sheet of baking paper and upturn the meringue on to it. Peel away the lining paper.
4 Spread the cream over the meringue and scatter with coffee beans. With a short end closest to you, lift the baking paper to roll up into a roulade. Lift onto a serving plate.
5 Melt the chocolate with the cream and drizzle over the meringue before serving.
Per serving: Cals 258, Fat 18g, Sat Fat 11g, Carbs 18g

Mixed spice parkin with apple and star anise

A rich and moist parkin with a wonderful aroma.

Serves 12 - Ready in 1 hr

* 4 star anise, plus extra for decorating
* 25 g | 0.8 oz caster sugar
* 225 g | 8.4 oz self-raising flour
* 1tsp ground mixed spice
* 1tsp bicarbonate of soda
* 100 g | 3.5 oz medium oatmeal
* 4 Russet or Cox's apples
* 2tsp lemon juice
* 100 g | 3.5 oz slightly salted butter
* 150 g | 5.3 oz black treacle, plus extra for drizzling
* 125 g | 4.4 oz golden syrup
* 50 ml | 1.7 fl oz milk
* 1 medium egg, beaten
* Demerara sugar, for sprinkling

1 Heat the oven to 150°C/300°F/ Gas Mark 2. Whizz the star anise in a spice grinder with the caster sugar until fine, then add to the flour, spice, bicarb and oatmeal.
2 Peel two of the apples and grate into the dry ingredients. Peel and slice the others and toss with lemon juice.
3 Heat the butter with the treacle and golden syrup until melted. Remove from heat and stir in the milk, then the egg. Stir into the dry ingredients, and pour into the tin. Scatter with apple slices and whole star anise.
4 Bake for 45 mins, until the centre feels just firm to the touch. Sprinkle with demerara sugar and serve warm or cold.
Per serving: Cals 280, Fat 9g, Sat Fat 5g, Carbs 45g

CHRISTMAS PUDDING 3 WAYS

Whatever your dietary needs we've the perfect pud

Citrus gluten-free pudding

This recipe makes 2 puddings – why not gift one to a friend?

Makes 2 x 900 g puddings, each serving 8 • Ready in 7 hrs

- ✳ **2 large lemons**
- ✳ **150 g | 5.3 oz gluten-free bread**
- ✳ **60 g | 2 oz gluten-free self-raising flour (we used Doves Farm)**
- ✳ **175 g | 6 oz dark muscovado sugar**
- ✳ **1tbsp mixed spice**
- ✳ **500 g | 17 oz dried mixed fruit**
- ✳ **250 g | 8.8 oz ready-to-eat prunes, chopped**
- ✳ **90 g | 3 oz grated carrot**
- ✳ **150 g | 5.3 oz chilled butter, grated**
- ✳ **60 g | 2 oz blanched almonds, chopped**
- ✳ **3 eggs**
- ✳ **150 ml | 5.3 oz cider**
- ✳ **5tbsp whisky**
- ✳ **3tbsp sherry**
- ✳ **1 orange, sliced**

YOU WILL NEED
- ✳ **2 x 1 iltre greased and base-lined pudding basins**
- ✳ **Baking parchment**
- ✳ **Foil**
- ✳ **String**

1 Put 1 lemon in a pan of cold water, cover and bring to the boil. Simmer for 30 mins until very soft. Drain and cool for a few mins.
2 Meanwhile, break the gluten-free bread into a processor and blitz to turn into breadcrumbs. Tip into a large bowl.
3 Quarter the softened lemon, remove seeds and blitz in a processor to finely chop. Tip into the bowl with the breadcrumbs.

4 Add the gluten-free flour, sugar, mixed spice, dried mixed fruit, prunes, carrot, butter and chopped almonds.
5 Combine the eggs in a jug with the cider, whisky and sherry and mix together with a fork. Pour into the bowl and mix everything together.
6 Slice the remaining lemon and arrange with the a slice or two of the orange at the base of each pudding

basin. Divide the mixture between the basins and smooth over. Cover with a double sheet of pleated baking paper and foil and secure with string.
7 Cook in a steamer for 6 hrs, checking and topping up with boiling water every 30 mins or as needed.
Per serving: Cals 303, Fat 11g, Sat Fat 5g, Carbs 41g

Vegan figgy puddings

Try this luxurious pud as part of your Christmas feast – no one will even know it's vegan!

Serves 8 • Ready in 5 hrs 30 mins

* Coconut oil, for greasing
* 90g | 3 oz plain flour
* 1tsp ground nutmeg
* 1tsp mixed spice
* 1tsp cinnamon
* 90 g | 3 oz dark muscovado sugar
* 45 g | 1.5 oz dry white breadcrumbs
* 100 g | 3.5 oz vegan suet
* ½ tsp baking powder
* 2tbsp black treacle
* 6tbsp almond milk, brandy or rum
* Grated zest and juice of 1 orange and 1 lemon
* 2tbsp beetroot powder
* 1 apple, grated
* 250 g | 8.8 oz mixed dried fruit
* 200 g | 7 oz dried figs, chopped to serve
* 5tbsp maple syrup
* 2tbsp rum
* Edible gold glitter
* 1 fig, cut into wedges

1 Grease and base-line eight individual pudding basins. Combine the flour, nutmeg, mixed spice, cinnamon, sugar, breadcrumbs, suet and baking powder in a large mixing bowl.
2 Add in the treacle, almond milk, brandy or rum, orange and lemon zest and juice, beetroot powder, apple and all the dried fruit into the flour mixture. Mix everything together with a spoon until all the ingredients are well combined.
3 Divide the sponge mixture equally between the small individual pudding basins.
Cover with a sheet of baking parchment and foil, both pleated in the middle, and secure with string. Steam for 4 hrs, topping up the water as needed.
4 To serve, warm the puddings through in the steamer for 1 hr. Warm the maple syrup and rum together, then sprinkle in some of the edible gold glitter.
5 Turn the puddings out onto plates, top each one with a fig wedge and drizzle over the warm, glittery maple syrup mixture.
Per serving: Cals 440, Fat 11.5g, Sat Fat 6g, Carbs 70g

Sherry-soaked Christmas pudding

Make an entrance with this flaming veggie Christmas pud!

Serves 8 • Ready in 7 hrs

* **150g | 5.3 oz each of currants, raisins, sultanas and prunes**
* **300ml | 10.5 oz Pedro Ximénez sherry**
* **4tbsp ginger wine**
* **Finely grated zest and juice of 1 orange**
* **90g | 3 oz molasses sugar**
* **45g | 1.5 oz self-raising flour**
* **2tsp ground mixed spice**
* **125g | 4.4 oz vegetable suet**
* **30g | 1 oz blanched almonds, chopped**
* **90g | 3 oz white breadcrumbs**
* **90g | 3 oz carrots, grated**
* **2 eggs**
* **1.25 litre pudding basin**
* **Baking parchment**
* **Foil**
* **String**

1 Put the dried fruits in a pan and pour in the sherry and ginger wine. Add the orange zest and juice. Cover and cook over a medium heat until the fruits are warm and have soaked up some of the liquid.

2 Pour the dried fruits and liquid into an airtight container and leave overnight to macerate. The following day, pour half of the dried fruit and liquid into a food processor and blend until smooth.

Crumble the molasses sugar into a large bowl, breaking up any lumps with your fingers. Sieve in the flour and mixed spice. Then stir in the suet and almonds.

3 Add the blended fruits along with the whole fruits and liquid. Stir in the breadcrumbs and grated carrot then, finally, the eggs. Mix everything together well.

4 Spoon the pudding mixture into the basin. Cover with a double sheet of baking parchment and foil, pleated in the middle, and secure with string.

5 Cook in a steamer for 6 hrs, checking the pan and topping up with boiling water every 30 mins or as needed.

Per serving: Cals 528, Fat 18g, Sat Fat 8.5g, Carbs 72g

Coconut cheesecake with tropical fruit

These look very cute when served!

Serves 6 • Ready in 30 mins, plus chilling

* 80 g | 2.8 oz butter
* 175 g | 6 oz ginger nut biscuits, crushed

FOR THE FILLING
* 4 sheets gelatine
* 2 x 160 ml | 5.5 fl oz tin coconut cream
* 150 g | 5.3 fl ozcaste sugar
* 300 g | 10.5 oz Philadelphia cream cheese, softened
* zest and juice of 2 limes
* 2 x 400 g | 14 oz tins fruit in juice
* 3tbsp toasted coconut flakes

1 Melt the butter in a pan and mix with the biscuit crumbs, then press into the bases of 6 x 8cm lightly oiled flan rings on a baking tray lined with foil. Chill for 20 mins.
2 Soak the gelatine for 4 mins in cold water. Meanwhile, gently heat the coconut cream and sugar, stirring until dissolved. Remove from heat. Squeeze any excess water from the gelatine and stir into hot cream to dissolve. Set aside to cool.
3 Beat the cream cheese, lime zest and juice in a bowl until smooth. Stir in the coconut mixture and whisk well. Carefully pour into the flan rings and chill for 3 hrs.
4 Whizz ½ the fruit and all the juice, sieve and drizzle over the cheesecakes. Top with the remaining fruit and toasted coconut.
Per serving: 689 cals, Fat 42g, Sat fat 30g, Carbs 69g

Rocky road Christmas pud

This no-bake Christmas dessert is fuss-free and great value if you're on a budget. Perfect for kids.

Serves 8 • Ready in 30 mins, plus 4 hrs chilling

* 200 g | 7 oz milk chocolate and 100g dark chocolate, broken into squares
* 4tbsp golden syrup
* 175g | 6 oz butter
* 175g | 6 oz digestive biscuits, broken into small pieces
* 125 g | 4.4 oz raisins
* 100 g | 3.5 oz glacé cherries, rinsed, dried and quartered
* melted chocolate, chocolate-covered raisins, cream-coloured sugar paste
* holly and icing sugar, to decorate

1 Line a 500ml pudding basin with cling film. Melt the milk and dark chocolates with the golden syrup and butter in a heatproof bowl over a pan of simmering water, making sure the water doesn't touch the bottom of the bowl.
2 Remove bowl from the pan. Stir in the biscuits, raisins and glacé cherries. Spoon into the lined basin, pressing down firmly. Chill for 4 hrs in the fridge until firm.
3 Turn the pudding out of the bowl and remove the cling film. Cover the pudding with melted chocolate and decorate with chocolate-covered raisins. Place a circle of sugar paste on the top, add a sprig of holly and a dusting of icing sugar.
Per serving: Cals 576, Fat 34g, Sat fat 20g, Carbs 62g

TIP
No citrus zester? Use the coarsest side of a cheese grater

Rosemary and lemon Bundt with gin glaze

A boozy showstopper that will wow all your guests.

Serves 14 • Ready in 1 hr 40 mins

* ✳ **300 g | 10.5 oz unsalted butter, melted, plus extra for greasing**
* ✳ **350 g | 12 oz caster sugar**
* ✳ **100 g | 3.5 oz runny honey**
* ✳ **4 eggs**
* ✳ **300 g | 10.5 oz Greek yogurt**
* ✳ **zest of 3 large lemons**
* ✳ **1tsp fresh rosemary leaves, chopped**
* ✳ **1tsp vanilla extract**
* ✳ **450 g | 15.8 oz plain flour**
* ✳ **2tsp baking powder**

FOR THE SYRUP
* ✳ **80 g | 2.8 oz sugar**
* ✳ **2tbsp lemon juice**
* ✳ **1tbsp gin**

FOR THE ICING
* ✳ **2tbsp gin**
* ✳ **200 g | 7 oz icing sugar, sifted**

FOR THE CANDIED ROSEMARY AND LEMON
* ✳ **200 g | 7 oz sugar**
* ✳ **4-6 sprigs fresh rosemary**
* ✳ **2 lemons, thinly sliced**

YOU WILL NEED
* ✳ **25 x 10.2 cm Bundt tin**

1 Heat the oven to 170°C/325°F/ Gas Mark 4. Grease the Bundt tin using melted butter. Whisk together the butter, sugar, honey, egg and yogurt with the lemon zest, rosemary and vanilla.

2 In a separate bowl, sieve the flour and baking powder. Fold the dry ingredients into the wet mixture. Spoon the mixture into the tin, put on a baking tray and cook for 1 hr. Transfer to a wire rack.

3 To make the syrup, put the sugar, lemon juice and gin, plus 80ml water, into a small saucepan and heat until the sugar has dissolved. While the cake is hot, brush the syrup all over the cake.

4 To make the candied rosemary, dissolve 100g sugar in 25ml water. Put the remaining sugar on a plate. Coat the rosemary in the liquid and then roll in the sugar. Place on a piece of parchment paper to dry out.

5 To make the candied lemon, heat the oven to 110°C/225°F/Gas Mark ¼. Add the lemon slices to the sugar mixture you used for the rosemary and coat both sides. Place the lemon slices on baking parchment and bake in 1 hr. Check every 20 mins to make sure they aren't burning. Once dry, remove any excess sugar and leave until ready to decorate.

6 Make the icing by mixing the gin and icing sugar. Drizzle over the cake and place the candied rosemary and lemon on top.

Per serving: Cals 530, Fat 21g, Sat fat 13g, Carbs 77g

TIP
You can make the candied rosemary and lemon ahead of time – simply store in an airtight container until ready to use

GREAT FOR VEGGIES

Golden cinnamon brownies

These delicious brownies have a hint of warming spice and can be transported easily for any festive gatherings.

Makes 10 • Ready in 1 hr

FOR THE BROWNIES
* **75 g | 2.6 oz dark chocolate,** broken into squares
* **100 g | 3.5 oz butter**
* **3 eggs**
* **325 g | 11 oz golden caster sugar**
* **2tsp vanilla extract**
* **125 g | 4.4 oz self-raising** flour, sieved
* **30 g | 1 oz cocoa**
* **2tsp cinnamon**
* **½tsp ground nutmeg**

TO DECORATE
* **edible gold leaf**
* **10 white chocolate stars**
* **1tbsp icing sugar**

1 Heat the oven to 180°C/350°F/Gas Mark 4, then grease and line a 23cm-round silicone segment mould. Melt the chocolate and butter in a heatproof bowl over a pan of simmering water.
2 Whisk together the eggs, sugar and vanilla extract with an electric mixer, until pale, thick and tripled in volume.
3 Fold the self-raising flour, cocoa, cinnamon, ground nutmeg and melted chocolate and butter into the egg and sugar mixture, until evenly combined.
4 Use an ice-cream scoop to divide the mixture equally between the sections of the segment mould. Bake for 15 mins, until the brownies are risen and firm. Leave to cool in the mould, then turn the segments out.
5 To decorate your brownies, use a small paintbrush to paint a bit of gold leaf in a random pattern on top of each one. Add a white chocolate star to the top of each segment.
6 Arrange the brownies in a star shape on a serving plate, then dust generously with icing sugar.
Per serving: Cals 341, Fat 13g, Sat fat 8g, Carbs 49g

TIP
Pop a small dipping bowl of cream in the centre as an alternative way to display

Christmas shortbread

With their delicate rose and almond flavour, these melt-in-the-mouth biscuits would make a lovely gift or tree decoration.

Makes 22-24 biscuits • Ready in 50 mins, plus chilling

* **150 g | 3.5 oz plain flour,** plus extra for dusting
* **25 g | 0.8 oz ground rice**
* **125 g | 4.4 oz firm slightly salted butter, diced**
* **½tsp rose extract**
* **75 g | 2.6 oz caster sugar**
* **small handful of unblanched almonds**
* **decorations, such as white icing, white sugar sprinkles, edible pearls, gold food colouring, chocolate and nuts**

1 Put the flour, rice and butter in a food processor and blend until the mixture resembles coarse breadcrumbs. Add the rose extract and sugar, and blend to a firm paste. Wrap and chill for at least 30 mins.
2 Heat the oven to 180°C/350°F/Gas Mark 4. Grease two baking trays. Roll out the dough on a floured surface to 5mm thickness. Cut out shapes and space slightly apart on the baking sheets – you could cut out stars from the middle of some rounds or press almonds into others. Use a skewer to make holes for hanging your biscuits.
3 Bake for 25 mins until the biscuits are turning gold around the edges. Re-mark the holes with a skewer if necessary. Cool, then decorate.
Per serving: 89-82 Cals, Fat 5-4.7g, Sat fat 3-2.8g, Carbs 10-9g

TIP
Add a light dusting of caster sugar for a snowy feel

Biscoff gingerbread cake

Merry Christmas

TIP
If you prefer, you could use 3 x 18cm-round cake tins for this cake – just adjust the baking time to 25 mins

Biscoff gingerbread cake

Get the flavours of the burnt caramel biscuits you find in posh hotels.

Serves 12-15 • Ready in 1 hr 15 mins, plus cooling

FOR THE CAKE
✳ **175 g | 6 oz butter, cubed**
✳ **150 g | 5.3 oz dark muscovado sugar**
✳ **3tbsp black treacle**
✳ **150 ml | 5.3 fl oz milk**
✳ **225 g | 8 oz plain flour, sifted**
✳ **1tbsp ground ginger**
✳ **1tsp bicarbonate of soda**
✳ **2 eggs, lightly beaten**

FOR THE FILLING
✳ **360 g | 12.6 oz cream cheese**
✳ **400 g | 14 oz Lotus Biscoff Spread**

TO DECORATE
✳ **210 g | 7 oz salted caramel, to spread**
✳ **25 g | 0.8 oz mini gingerbread men**

1 Heat the oven to 200°C/400°F/Gas Mark 6, then grease and baseline 5x15cm round cake tins or a layer-cake pan set.
2 Put the butter, sugar, treacle and milk in a pan. Heat gently until melted, stirring. Add the flour, ginger and bicarb of soda. Slowly mix in the eggs.
3 Split between the tins. Bake for 20 mins. Remove from the oven. Leave to cool slightly. Remove from the tins and cool completely on wire racks.
4 Blend the cream cheese and Biscoff spread. Sandwich the 5 cakes with thin layers of the mixture. Place the cake on a stand and spread a thin layer of mixture around the sides and top.
5 Fit a piping bag with a large star nozzle and fill with the remaining mixture. Set aside. Spoon the caramel spread into a disposable piping bag, snip off the end and pipe around the edge of the cake to create a drip effect down its sides. Pipe the remaining caramel in the centre of the cake.
6 Pipe swirls of Biscoff mixture around the edge. Stick the gingerbread men on top. Insert your topper. Chill, but bring to room temperature for serving.
Per serving: Cals 616-493, Fat 38-31g, Sat fat 18-14g, Carbs 60-48g

Chocolate orange Christmas cake

Convert Christmas cake sceptics with this chocolate orange take.

Serves 12 · Ready in 4 hrs 30 mins, plus soaking time

* ✳ **100 g | 3.5 oz mixed peel**
* ✳ **500 g | 17 oz mixed fruit**
* ✳ **5tbsp Cointreau/Grand Marnier**
* ✳ **juice of 1 orange**
* ✳ **200 g | 7 oz butter**
* ✳ **150 g | 5.3 oz light muscovado sugar**
* ✳ **50 g | 1.7 oz cocoa powder**
* ✳ **3 eggs, beaten**
* ✳ **100 g | 3.5 oz ground almonds**
* ✳ **175 g | 6 oz self-raising flour**
* ✳ **1tbsp mixed spice**

1 Soak the dried fruit in brandy/ Grand Marnier and the juice of 1 orange the day before you plan to make the cake.
2 Heat the oven to 130°C/250°F/ Gas Mark ½.
3 To prep the tin: grease and line a high-topped 18cm circle cake tin. Wrap a double layer of baking paper around the outside of the tin, so that it reaches several inches above the top of the tin. Secure with string.
4 Put the butter, sugar, cocoa powder into a pan and place on a medium heat until melted and then stir to combine. Leave cool for 10 mins. In a large mixing bowl, combine the beaten eggs, flour, ground almonds and mixed spice with a wooden spoon or spatula – however you like – to combine. Pour in the butter mixture and the dried fruit mixture and combine.
5 Pour the fruit cake mixture into the prepared cake tin. Place in the oven and bake for 1¾-2¼ hrs, by which time the top of the cake should be firm but will have a shiny and sticky look. If you insert a cake tester into the centre of the cake, it should come out clean while the surface of the cake should feel firm to the touch.
6 Put the cake on a cooling rack. It will hold its heat and take a while to cool, but once it has, unmould it from the tin and, if you don't want to eat it immediately (and like any fruit cake it has a very long life), wrap it in baking parchment and then in foil and place in a tin.

FOR THE CANDIED ORANGE PEEL
* ✳ **1 orange**
* ✳ **200 g | 7 oz sugar**
* ✳ **100 g | 3.5 oz dark chocolate, melted**

1 Place the whole orange in a pan of cold water and bring to the boil.
2 Remove and cool. Cut off each end and discard, cut the rest into 5mm thick rounds, cut the largest ones in half. Bring the sugar and 200ml water to the boil. Add the orange pieces and reduce to a gentle simmer with the lid on for 30 mins then remove the lid and continue to simmer for about 1 hr or until the pith begins to turn translucent. Stir intermittently to ensure they don't stick together.
3 Remove the orange pieces from the liquid and transfer to a cooling rack and dry overnight. Once firm dip into the melted chocolate.

FOR THE ICING
* ✳ **150g | 5.3 oz dark chocolate**
* ✳ **75 g | 2.6 oz cream**

Melt the chocolate, heat the cream, mix together. If it's splitting, add a dash of boiling water. Allow to cool to a thick but pourable consistency.

TO ASSEMBLE
* ✳ **2tbsp apricot jam, warmed**
* ✳ **500 g | 17 oz marzipan**

Place the cake on a serving dish. Spread the apricot jam over the top of the cake. Roll the marzipan into a circle on a lightly dusted surface so that it will fit on the top of the cake. Place it on top of the cake. Pour the chocolate icing over the top, allowing it to spill over the sides of the cake a little. Top with the orange slices.
Per serving: Cals 835, Fat 33g, Sat fat 15g, Carbs 116g

TIP
You could top the cake with a Terry's chocolate orange instead of the candied orange slices, to save time

Gluten-free Florentine cake

This cake is almost as fun to decorate as it is to eat.

Serves 12 • Ready in 1 hr 10 mins

* 6 large eggs
* 220 g | 7.5 oz caster sugar
* 200 g | 7 oz cornflour
* 100 g | 3.5 oz glacé cherries, to decorate
* 100 g | 3.5 oz marshmallows, to decorate

FOR THE FILLING
* 200 g | 7 oz egg white
* 400 g | 14 oz caster sugar
* 500 g | 17 oz unsalted butter
* 1tsp vanilla extract

FOR THE FLORENTINES
* 25 g | 0.8 oz butter
* 100 g | 3.5 oz light muscovado sugar
* 1tbsp crème fraîche
* 75 g | 2.6 oz roasted, salted mixed nuts, chopped
* 25 g | 0.8 oz red glacé cherries
* 1tsp vanilla extract
* 150 g | 5.3 oz dark chocolate

YOU WILL ALSO NEED
* 3 x 20cm round cake tins, greased and lined

1 For the Florentines, melt the butter in a pan and add the sugar and 1tbsp of water, then stir until the sugar dissolves. Bring to the boil, then simmer for 5-7 mins until the mixture thickens slightly. Add the crème fraîche and simmer for a further 2-3 mins.

2 To test whether the mixture will set, spoon a small amount onto a plate and place in the fridge for a few mins. If it feels firm to the touch, it's cooked enough, but if it is still very soft, simmer for a few more mins and then repeat the test.

3 Remove from the heat and stir in the nuts, cherries and vanilla. Place small spoonfuls of the mixture onto a board lined with baking parchment and leave the cool and set.

4 Spoon circles of melted chocolate onto a board lined with baking parchment. Lift up one of the Florentines and place it on top. Repeat for the others, working one at a time, then leave to set.

5 For the cake, heat the oven to 180°C/350°F/Gas Mark 4. Beat the eggs with the caster sugar until light and fluffy and the whisk leaves a ribbon trail when lifted out of the mixture. Sieve the cornflour into the mixture and fold it in gently. Divide the batter between the cake tins and bake for 15-18 mins until golden brown. Remove from the tins and allow to cool on a wire rack.

6 For the icing, pour the egg whites into a bowl and add the sugar and a pinch of salt. Place the bowl over a pan of summering water, and stir with a whisk or spoon. Stir until the sugar crystals have dissolved. If you put your finger and thumb into the mixture and lift them out, when you rub them together you should not feel any graininess.

7 Whisk the egg white mixture until it's a very thick meringue, and continue to whisk until it cools and the bowl feels slightly warm. Gradually whisk in the butter, a small knob at a time.

8 Keep whisking until the mixture thickens. To begin with, it may look like it has collapsed and curdled, but keep whisking on a high speed until it forms a thick smooth buttercream. Scrape down the sides of the bowl and beat the mixture again. Add the vanilla to taste.

9 Place one of the sponges on a serving plate, and spread over a third of the icing. Repeat with the remaining icing and 2 sponges. Place the Florentines around the edge of the cake and continue to decorate, as you wish, with the cherries and marshmallows.

Per serving: Cals 844, Fat 46g, Sat fat 27g, Carbs 97g

TIP
Use any type of chocolate that you like to dip the Florentines

GREAT FOR VEGGIES, LOW CALORIE

Raspberry and blackcurrant meringue log

Melt-in-the-mouth marshmallowy meringue smothered with creamy Greek yogurt, delicious blackcurrant curd and tangy raspberries.

Serves 12 • Ready in 1 hr 20 mins

* **5 large egg whites**
* **150 g | 5.3 oz golden caster sugar**
* **2tsp cornflour**
* **25 g | 0.8 oz icing sugar, to dust**
* **500 g | 17 oz 0% fat Total Greek yogurt**
* **340 g | 12 oz blackcurrant curd (we used Tiptree)**
* **200 g | 7 oz raspberries**

TO DECORATE
* **holly leaves**
* **extra icing sugar, to dust**

1 Heat the oven to 150°C/300°F/Gas Mark 2. Line a 30cm x 20cm Swiss roll tin with baking parchment.
2 Using an electric whisk, whisk the egg whites to stiff peaks, then gradually add in the caster sugar until the mixture is stiff and glossy. Whisk in the cornflour.
3 Spread the meringue evenly in the prepared Swiss roll tin. Bake for 1 hr. Leave to cool completely in the tin.
4 Lay a sheet of baking parchment on the work surface and sprinkle with sieved icing sugar. Turn the meringue upside down onto the sugar-dusted paper and peel away the baking parchment.
5 Spread Greek yogurt over the meringue. Spoon over the blackcurrant curd and sprinkle on the raspberries.
6 With one of the long ends of the meringue closest to you, lift the parchment to carefully roll into a roulade. Lift onto a serving plate with a palette knife. Decorate with holly leaves. Dust with icing sugar to serve.
Per serving: Cals 173, Fat 1.5g, Sat fat 0.4g, Carbs 33g

TIP
Serve with a dollop or two of extra Greek yogurt for freshness

Chocolate and raspberry roulade

Add some festive cheer with this twist on a classic roulade.

Serves 16 • Ready in 1 hr, plus cooling

FOR THE ROULADE
* **200 g | 7 oz white chocolate, broken into squares**
* **6 large eggs, separated**
* **175 g | 6 oz golden caster sugar**

FOR THE FILLING
* **300 ml | 10.5 double cream, whipped**
* **2tbsp icing sugar**
* **1tbsp vanilla bean paste**
* **4tbsp golden caster sugar**
* **6tbsp seedless raspberry jam**
* **250 g | 8.8 oz fresh raspberries to decorate**
* **90 g | 3 oz white chocolate**
* **1tsp sunflower oil**
* **¼tsp edible gold glitter**

1 Heat the oven to 180°C/350°F/ Gas Mark 4 and grease and line a 38cm x 26cm Swiss roll tin with baking parchment.
2 Gently melt the white chocolate in a heatproof bowl over a pan of simmering water.
3 Meanwhile, whisk the egg whites in a clean, grease-free bowl, until they are softly peaking.
4 In another bowl, whisk together the egg yolks and golden caster sugar using an electric mixer, until they are pale and thick.
5 Take the chocolate off the heat and stir until smooth, then beat into the egg yolks. Gently fold in the egg whites to combine. Pour the mixture into the tin and bake for 25 mins.
6 Remove the roulade from the oven and covered with a clean, damp tea towel. Leave to cool.
7 For the filling, whisk together the cream, icing sugar and vanilla bean paste until peaking.
8 Sprinkle the caster sugar onto a sheet of baking parchment. Turn out the roulade onto it and peel away the baking parchment. Trim the edges of the roulade to neaten. Spread the jam onto the roulade, followed by the cream. Add the raspberries. Roll up the roulade tightly, from the shortest side, lifting up the paper to help, then chill in the fridge.
9 To decorate, place the white chocolate and the oil in a bowl over a pan of simmering water. Once melted, spoon into a piping bag, snip off the end and drizzle over the roulade. Top the roulade with icing sugar, edible glitter and any decoration you like. This will keep for four days in the fridge.
Per serving: Cals 303, Fat 18g, Sat fat 10g, Carbs 29g

White forest gateau

A stunning cake fit for a snow queen, made super easy with a red-velvet ready mix.

Serves 16 • Takes 1 hr 15 mins, plus cooling

* **425 g | 15 oz packet Betty Crocker**
* **Red Velvet Cake Mix**
* **65 ml | 2 oz vegetable oil**
* **3 eggs**
* **500 g | 17 oz mascarpone cheese**
* **2tbsp cherry liqueur**
* **300 g | 10.5 oz black cherry jam**
* **425 g | 15 oz can pitted black cherries, drained and chopped**

FOR THE FROSTING
* **3 large egg whites**
* **250 g | 8.8 oz caster sugar**
* **white chocolate curls, chocolate pine cones and icing sugar, to decorate**

1 Heat oven to 180°C/350°F/Gas Mark 4. Grease and line 5 x 15cm round cake tins (such as Wilton Easy Layer Cake Pan Set, Lakeland). Make up the cake mix with oil, water and eggs, following the packet instructions. Divide the mixture between the tins and bake for 20 mins until just firm to the touch. Turn out of the tins and leave to cool completely on a wire rack.
2 Beat the mascarpone and liqueur together until soft and smooth. Sandwich the cakes together with the jam, cherries and mascarpone.
3 For the frosting, put the egg whites and sugar in a bowl over a pan of gently simmering water and stir until the sugar has dissolved.
4 Remove the bowl from the pan and, using an electric whisk, beat the mixture until it becomes thick like a meringue.
5 Spread the meringue frosting over the top and sides of the cake. Pile white chocolate curls and chocolate pine cones on top, and dust with icing sugar.
Per serving: Cals 412, Fat 21g, Sat fat 12g, Carbs 51g

TIP
You can also make the leaves using green fondant

Your perfect
CHRISTMAS CAKE

Basic Christmas cake recipe

Create the perfect centrepiece for your celebrations with our easy fruit cake recipe, and choose from a number of easy, yet eye-catching decorating options.

Serves 12 • Ready in 3 hrs 5 mins

✳ 3 large eggs
✳ 300 g | 10.5 oz plain flour
✳ 250 g | 8.8 oz butter
✳ 250 g | 8.8 oz light muscovado sugar
✳ 1tbsp mixed spice
✳ 410 g | 14 oz jar mincemeat
✳ 500 g | 17 oz dried mixed fruit
✳ 4tbsp brandy
✳ 4tbsp apricot jam, warmed
✳ 750 g | 26 oz marzipan
✳ 1 kg | 2.2 lb white sugar paste

1 Heat the oven to 140°C/275°F/Gas Mark 1. Mix together the eggs, flour, butter, sugar, mixed spice, salt, mincemeat and fruit in a bowl. Beat until smooth. Grease and line a 20cm round cake tin with parchment. Pour in the cake mix and smooth over.
2 Bake for 3 hrs or until the cake feels firm to touch and a skewer inserted comes out clean. Leave to cool for 15 mins, drizzle over the brandy and leave to cool completely in the tin. Then see pages 128 and 129 for how to create your favourite decorating style.
Per serving: Cals 1,129, Fat 29g, Sat fat 12g, Carbs 202g

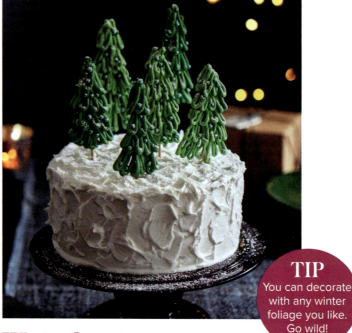

TIP
You can decorate with any winter foliage you like. Go wild!

Winter forest

Top your cake with a snowy scene.

Serves 12 • Ready in 15 mins, plus overnight drying

✳ 300 g | 10.5 oz icing sugar, plus extra for dusting
✳ 500 g | 17 oz golden marzipan
✳ 2tbsp apricot jam
✳ 50 g | 1.7 oz egg whites
✳ green food colouring
✳ dragee balls
YOU ALSO WILL NEED
✳ 6 x kebab sticks

1 Dust a surface with icing sugar. Roll the marzipan out to 3mm thick, large enough to cover the cake. Warm the jam and spread over the top and sides of the cake. Lay the marzipan over and smooth using your hands.
2 Put the sugar and egg white into the bowl of an electric mixer, cover the bowl with a tea towel, and mix with the paddle attachment on a low speed for 5 mins.
3 Spread the icing over the cake (you will have some left over). Use the back of a spoon to create a texture by pulling it away from the cake.
4 Add green colour to the remaining icing and put into a piping bag, snip the end off. Arrange the sticks on a tray lined with baking parchment and use the green icing to pipe trees over the sticks. Press a few dragee balls into each and allow to dry overnight.
5 Once set hard, peel the baking parchment away from the trees and push them into the cake. Dust with icing sugar to look like fresh snow.

Traditional holly

For a classic look, try this holly decoration.

Serves 12 • Ready in 15 mins

* 4tbsp apricot jam, warmed
* 750 g | 26 oz marzipan
* 1 kg | 2.2 lb white fondant icing
* icing sugar, to dust
* edible glue
* edible holly decoration

YOU WILL ALSO NEED

* ribbon of your choice

1 Brush the jam over the top and sides of the cake. Roll out the marzipan on a surface lightly dusted with icing sugar so it's big enough to cover the top and sides of the cake. Smooth down the marzipan with an icing smoother. Trim any excess.

2 Roll out the fondant icing so it is large enough to cover the cake. Brush water all over the marzipan and carefully cover with the fondant icing. Use the icing smoother to smooth the edges and trim away excess.

3 Use the edible glue to stick the holly decorations in a circle around the top of the cake to finish. Measure the ribbon to fit around the bottom edge of the cake, with a little overhang. Pin it into place at the join.

TIP
Warming the apricot jam makes it a lot easier to brush over

TIP
If you don't have a blowtorch, you could place the cake under a hot grill

Marzipan festive star

Let the marzipan be the centrepiece with this beautiful caramelised decoration that's bound to impress.

Serves 12 • Ready in 20 mins

* 3tbsp apricot jam, warmed
* 1 kg | 2.2 lb marzipan
* 2 tbsp dark molasses sugar (optional)

YOU WILL ALSO NEED

* large star cookie cutter or template
* smaller star cookie cutter or template.

1 Brush the top of the cake with apricot jam. Roll the marzipan out on a surface that is lightly dusted with icing sugar so that you have enough to cover the top of the cake and cut out both of the stars. Use the base of the tin that you baked the cake in, to measure a circle. Rest this marzipan circle on the top of the cake.

2 Either by using a cookie cutter or by using a sharp knife around a template cut out the 2 star sizes from the remaining marzipan. Use a knife to score the smaller star from the centre outwards. Brush water across one side of both stars; lay the larger star down first on top of the cake and the second star on top of it. Using any remaining marzipan roll out a small ball and stick this down in the middle of the smaller star with water.

3 Sprinkle the dark molasses sugar on top of the marzipan and then carefully caramelise the sugar with a blowtorch (optional).

Chocolate fridge wreath

A little goes a long way with this super-rich fridge cake.

Serves 32 • Ready in 40 mins, plus chilling

* **300 g | 10.5 oz Belgian milk chocolate, cubed**
* **180 g | 6.3 oz bar dark chocolate**
* **6tbsp golden syrup**
* **200 g | 7 oz butter, at room temperature**
* **225 g | 7.8 oz packet marshmallows, quartered**
* **300 g | 10.5 oz gingernut biscuits, crushed**
* **240 g | 8.4 oz chocolate digestives, broken into pieces**

TO DECORATE

* **15 clean, dry bay leaves**
* **edible silver lustre spray**
* **180 g | 6.3 oz bar dark chocolate**
* **2tsp vegetable oil**
* **lustred chocolate balls**
* **edible silver glitter**

YOU WILL ALSO NEED

* **empty, recycled food can, greased on the outside and wrapped in baking paper**
* **23cm spring-clip tin, greased and lined**
* **clean dishcloth**

1 Put the milk and dark chocolates into a large bowl with the syrup and butter. Heat over a pan of simmering water until melted and smooth.
2 Remove the pan from the heat, stir in the marshmallows, gingernuts and pieces of chocolate digestive.
3 Position the can in the centre of the cake tin and spoon the chocolate mixture around it. Press down the top to level and chill for 30 mins.

4 For the decoration, spread the bay leaves out on a paper-lined baking tray. Spray with edible silver lustre and leave to dry. Melt the chocolate and oil in a heatproof bowl over a pan of simmering water.
5 Put the dishcloth into a bowl of very hot water. Wearing rubber gloves, squeeze out the excess moisture. Pack the cloth into the centre of the can and leave for a few mins. Remove the cloth and twist the can. Remove the cake from the tin and put on a plate or cake stand.
6 Spoon the melted chocolate over the top of the cake to cover, letting it drizzle down the side. Arrange the bay leaves and chocolate balls in clusters on top and dust with edible silver glitter to finish.
Per serving: Cals 230, Fat 13g, Sat fat 8g, Carbs 25g

TIP
This is the perfect gift for chocoholic friends and looks attractive packed in a box tied with a ribbon bow

TIP
Yuzu juice is from a Japanese citrus fruit. It tastes like a mix of lime, grapefruit and satsuma. You can buy it in small bottles in Waitrose and specialist grocers. Tastes amazing on fish and in vodka cocktails

Winter fruit salad with coconut sorbet

Winter fruit salad with coconut sorbet

A refreshingly tropical dessert to clean the palate after indulging in a big meal.

Serves 6 • Ready in 1hr 20 mins, plus freezing

FOR THE SORBET
* **150 ml | 3.5 fl oz caster sugar**
* **1 vanilla pod**
* **finely grated zest and juice of 1 lime**
* **140 g | 3.2 fl oz tube liquid glucose**
* **500 ml | 17 fl oz coconut cream**
* **200 ml | 7 fl oz coconut milk**

FOR THE FRUIT SALAD
* **6 satsumas, peeled**
* **300 ml | 10.5 fl oz caster sugar**
* **3 star anise**
* **3 cloves**
* **thickly cut zest of ½ a lemon**
* **3tbsp yuzu juice**
* **1 pineapple, skin removed and cut into chunks**
* **2 mangoes, peeled and cut into chunks**
* **3 passion fruit**

YOU WILL ALSO NEED
* **Ice-cream maker**

1 In a small pan, heat the sugar with 150ml water, the vanilla and lime zest and juice until the sugar has dissolved. Add the liquid glucose, continue to heat and mix until combined. Set aside to cool.
2 Discard the vanilla, then mix the syrup base with the coconut cream and milk until smooth. Churn in an ice-cream maker until set. Freeze until ready to use.

3 For the fruit salad, place the satsumas in a bowl of boiling water for 2 mins, drain, allow to cool slightly and peel off any remaining pith, then set aside.
4 In a small pan, gently heat the sugar with 300ml water, the star anise, cloves and lemon zest until the sugar has dissolved, then set aside to cool.
5 Up to 2 hours before serving, mix the yuzu with the syrup until combined. Add the prepared fruit and passion-fruit seeds, and mix to coat. Serve with a scoop of the coconut sorbet.
Per serving: Cals 688, Fat 21g, Sat fat 18g, Carbs 122g

Extra-fruity Christmas pudding

If you haven't made your pudding, this is the perfect no-fuss recipe, as it doesn't need time to mature.

Serves 6 • Ready in 3 hrs 15 mins, plus soaking

* **100 g | 3.5 oz dried apricots, finely chopped**
* **100 g | 3.5 oz dried cranberries**
* **200 g | 7 oz sultanas, raisins or currants**
* **100 g | 3.5 oz ready-to-eat pitted prunes, finely chopped**
* **75 g | 2.6 oz blanched almonds**
* **50 g | 1.7 oz chopped mixed peel**
* **50 g | 1.7 oz candied ginger, finely chopped**
* **1 Bramley apple, coarsely grated**
* **grated zest of 1 lemon**
* **grated zest and juice of 1 orange**
* **100 ml | 3.5 fl oz spiced rum**
* **75 g | 2.6 oz unsalted butter**
* **75 g | 2.6 oz dark muscovado sugar (we used Billington's)**
* **1 large egg, lightly beaten**
* **125 g | 4.4 oz self-raising flour**
* **1tsp each mixed spice, ground nutmeg and ground cinnamon**
* **cranberries and bay or holly leaves, to decorate (optional)**

YOU WILL ALSO NEED
* **1.2 litre pudding basin**

1 In a large bowl, combine all the ingredients up to and including the spiced rum. Leave to soak overnight.
2 Soften the butter, then beat it with the sugar in a large bowl until light and fluffy. Slowly beat in the egg, a little at a time, until combined. Fold in the soaked fruit and the other remaining ingredients.
3 Lightly butter the pudding basin and fill with the prepared mixture. Cover with a double layer of buttered foil, making a pleat in the centre to allow for the pudding to rise. Tie string tightly around the basin rim to secure the foil.
4 Place in a pan and pour in enough water to that it comes halfway up the sides of the bowl. Cover with a tight-fitting lid and simmer for 3 hrs, topping up with water if necessary.
5 Remove the pan from the heat and leave uncovered for 15 mins before removing the foil and turning out the pudding. If making in advance, let it cool in the basin, then cover with clingfilm and chill in the fridge until needed.
6 To reheat the pudding, cover with foil and steam for 45 mins or cover with clingfilm, pierce holes in the top and microwave on high for 5 mins. Decorate with cranberries and bay or holly leaves, if using.
Per serving: Cals 589, Fat 19g, Sat fat 7.5g, Carbs 78g

Any leftover fruit salad can be served for breakfast the next day with granola and yogurt

TIP
This can be made ahead and stored for up to 1 week in the fridge

Festive chocolate, cherry and gingerbread trifle

Serves 20 • Ready in 2 hrs plus setting and cooling

FOR THE JELLY
* **1 pack black cherry jelly (we used Hartley's)**

FOR THE GINGER SPONGE
* **225 ml | 8.2 fl oz milk**
* **100 g | 3.5 oz light brown soft sugar**
* **100 g | 3.5 oz treacle**
* **110 g | 3.7 oz golden syrup**
* **zest of 1 orange**
* **55 g | 1.8 oz stem ginger in syrup, chopped**
* **110 g | 3.7 oz butter**
* **1 egg**
* **225 g | 8.2 oz self-raising flour**
* **1tsp bicarbonate of soda**
* **½tbsp ground ginger**
* **1tsp cinnamon**
* **½tsp ground mixed spice**

FOR THE CUSTARD
* **500 ml | 17 fl oz milk**
* **1tbsp vanilla bean paste**
* **75 g | 2.6 oz caster sugar**
* **6 egg yolks**
* **5tbsp cornflour**
* **100 g | 3.5 oz dark chocolate, melted**

FOR LAYERING & DECORATION
* **600 ml | 21 fl oz double cream**
* **460 g | 16 oz jar black cherries with kirsch, drained**
* **200 g | 7 oz fresh cherries or jar pitted cherries**
* **gold leaf and sparklers (optional)**

YOU WILL ALSO NEED
* **1 loaf tin**
* **1 large trifle bowl**

1 The night before, make the jelly according to packet instructions and leave to set in the fridge overnight.
2 The next day, heat the oven to 170°C/325°F/Gas Mark 3. Grease and line the loaf tin.

3 Heat the milk, brown sugar, treacle, syrup, orange zest and chopped stem ginger and stir until the sugar has dissolved. Remove from the heat and stir in the butter until melted. Whisk in the egg.
4 Sift the flour, bicarb of soda and spices into the milky mixture and whisk. Pour in the loaf tin and bake for 45 mins to 1 hr until a skewer comes out clean. Leave to cool then cut in to rough cubes (about 4cm).
5 While cooling make the custard: heat the milk and vanilla bean paste in a pan over a medium heat and bring it to a simmer.
6 Meanwhile, whisk together the sugar, egg yolks, cornflour and a pinch of salt in a bowl until you've a thick, smooth mix.
7 Remove the milk from the heat and, while constantly whisking, slowly pour about a quarter of the hot milk into the egg mix, add this milky egg mix back into the hot milk in the pan.
8 Heat the egg and milk mixture, whisking constantly, until it starts to thicken. Let the mixture boil for 1 min while stirring. Remove from the heat and mix in the melted chocolate Let the custard cool completely.
9 To assemble the trifle: whisk the double cream until soft peaks have formed. Remove the trifle bowl with jelly from the fridge, scatter over a layer of black cherries and ginger cake cubes. Give the chocolate custard a whisk to loosen it and pour half of it over the cherries and cake layer, followed by ½ the double cream. Repeat with another layer of cherries and cake, chocolate custard and double cream. Top with a dramatic scattering of gingerbread and fresh cherries (or pitted cherries). Decorate with gold leaf and 3 festive sparklers, if using.
Per serving: Cals 423, Fat 26g, Sat fat 15g, Carbs 43g

Snowy chocolate yule log

Doubles as a cake or dessert and so much nicer than a shop-bought pud.

Serves 10 • Ready in 45 mins, plus cooling

* **3 medium eggs**
* **100 g | 3.5 oz caster sugar**
* **55 g | 1.7 oz plain flour**
* **55 g | 1.7 oz ground almonds**
* **½tsp baking powder**
* **150 ml | 5.3 fl oz double cream**
* **200 g | 7 oz dark chocolate, melted**
* **2tbsp Irish cream liqueur, such as Baileys (optional)**
* **2tsp vanilla paste**
* **125 g | 4.4 oz Marshmallow Fluff**
* **150 g | 5.3 oz full-fat soft cheese**
* **Cocoa powder, to dust**

YOU WILL ALSO NEED
* **20 x 30cm Swiss roll tin, greased and lined**

1 Heat the oven to 180°C/350°F/Gas Mark 4. Whisk the eggs and sugar together, using an electric whisk, for 3-4 mins until very thick and pale.
2 Sift in the flour, almonds and baking powder, then fold in gently until just mixed. Spoon the mixture into the tin, spreading it evenly.
Bake for 12-15 mins, until golden and slightly springy to the touch. Cover with a clean, damp tea towel and leave to cool.
3 Whip the cream until thick enough to form soft peaks. Add the melted chocolate, cream liqueur and 1tsp vanilla paste and whisk to combine.
4 In a separate bowl, whisk together the Marshmallow Fluff, soft cheese and the remaining vanilla paste.
5 Turn the sponge out onto a large clean sheet of baking paper dusted with icing sugar and peel off the lining paper. Spread the chocolate cream over the cake, leaving a 3cm margin along one of the short sides, then roll up gently from the opposite edge, using the paper to help you.
6 Transfer rolled-up sponge to a serving plate. Spread the marshmallow frosting over to cover, creating a bark effect with a fork. Dust with a little cocoa powder and serve or chill for up to 24 hrs.
Per serving: Cals 413, Fat 26g, Sat fat 14g, Carbs 31g

TIP
For the best sponge, use eggs at room temperature and make sure you whisk the eggs and sugar until thick enough to write the letter 'M' on the surface of the mixture with the beaters

TIP
Although not in season you might find fresh redcurrants in the shops around Christmas. If not, you can use frozen redcurrants or switch to cranberries

Individual tiramisu

Always a winner and served in dainty glasses it looks stylish too.

Serves 6 • Ready in 20 mins

* **500 g | 17 oz** mascarpone cheese
* **85 g | 2.8 oz caster sugar**
* **25 g | 0.8 oz dark chocolate,** finely grated
* **3 tsp instant coffee granules**
* **100 ml | 3.5 fl oz Tia Maria**
TO DECORATE
* **24 Amaretti biscuits, plus 6 extra, make sure they are gluten free**

1 Beat the mascarpone until soft, then beat in the sugar. Reserve 1tbsp grated chocolate and stir the rest into the mascarpone.
2 Dissolve the coffee in 1tbsp boiling water and add the Tia Maria. Put the biscuits – reserving 6 for the decoration – on a deep plate, pour over the coffee mixture and leave to soak for 1 min. Put a soaked biscuit in the bottom of the 6 serving glasses and add 1tsp of the coffee liquid to each glass.
3 Divide half the mascarpone mixture between the glasses and top with the remaining soaked biscuits. Spoon on the rest of the mascarpone and pour over the remaining coffee mixture.
4 Top each glass with an Amaretti biscuit and sprinkle over the reserved chocolate.
Per serving: Cals 669, Fat 48g, Sat fat 27g, Carbs 44g

Redcurrant and honeycomb panna cotta

This combination of flavours and textures makes a delicious dessert.

Serves 4 • Ready in 20 mins, plus chilling

* **3 sheets leaf gelatine**
* **300 ml | 10.5 fl oz single cream**
* **200 ml | 7 fl oz full-fat milk**
* **2½tbsp runny honey**
FOR THE COMPOTE
* **200 g | 7 oz redcurrants**
* **45 g | 1.5 oz caster sugar**
TO FINISH
* **30 g | 1 oz honeycomb,** broken up

1 Soak the gelatine leaves in cold water for 10 mins, to soften.

2 Gently heat the cream, milk and honey in a small pan until very warm, but not boiling. Take off the heat. Remove the gelatine from the water and squeeze out excess water, add to the hot cream and stir until dissolved.
3 Strain through a fine sieve, then pour into 4 glasses. Place in the fridge for a least 4 hrs until set.
4 Heat the redcurrants, sugar and 2tsp water in a pan until thick and syrupy, with some currants still whole. Set aside to cool.
5 When ready to serve, spoon the fruit over the panna cotta and scatter over a few pieces of honeycomb.
Per serving: Cals 300, Fat 17g, Sat fat 10g, Carbs 32g

Look for award-winning Odysea honey in Waitrose. Hand-harvested in Greece, it's kind to bees

Chocolate, ginger and pistachio torte

Gluten free, nutty and tastes totally scrumptious, this sweet treat is a delight!

Serves 16 • Ready in 1 hr, plus cooling

✳ **510 g | 17.3 oz dark chocolate, broken into squares**
✳ **250 g | 8.8 oz butter, cut into 8 pieces**
✳ **6 large eggs, separated**
✳ **200 g | 7 oz golden caster sugar**
✳ **100 g | 3.5 oz shelled, unsalted pistachios**
✳ **4 balls stem ginger from a jar, finely chopped**
✳ **Cocoa powder, to dust**

YOU WILL ALSO NEED
✳ **23cm round cake tin, lined with baking paper**

1 Heat the oven to 180°C/350°F/ Gas Mark 4. Melt the chocolate and butter in a bowl over a pan of simmering water.
2 Place the egg yolks and sugar into a large bowl and whisk with an electric mixer for 5 mins, until pale, thick and creamy. Stir through the melted chocolate and butter, the pistachios and ginger.
3 In a clean bowl, whisk the egg whites until thick enough to form stiff peaks. Gently fold into the chocolate mixture.
4 Spoon the mixture into the lined tin and bake for 45 mins until just firm to the touch. Leave to cool in the tin.
5 To serve, dust heavily with cocoa powder. For extra decoration, you could place a star template on top.
Per serving: Cals 417, Fat 27g, Sat fat 15g, Carbs 35g

TIP
Good to keep in the freezer for when unexpected guests arrive. Once cooled, wrap in clingfilm and freeze. Defrost before dusting with cocoa powder, to serve

Nougat cheesecake

Great for feeding a crowd and you can make it up to 2 days ahead!

Serves 15 • Ready in 20 mins, plus setting

- ✳ **100 g | 3.5 oz unsalted butter**
- ✳ **225 g | 4 oz digestive biscuits, crushed**
- ✳ **4 gelatine leaves**
- ✳ **1 kg | 2.2 lb mascarpone**
- ✳ **400 g | 14 oz full-fat soft cheese**
- ✳ **150 g | 5.3 oz icing sugar, sifted**
- ✳ **125 g | 4.4 oz mixed toasted nuts (such as pistachios and hazelnuts)**
- ✳ **75 g | 2.6 oz nougat pieces, finely chopped**
- ✳ **1tsp vanilla extract**

TO DECORATE
- ✳ **hard almond nougat or brittle, broken into shards**
- ✳ **small handful pistachios, finely chopped**
- ✳ **small handful nougat pieces, cut into cubes**
- ✳ **edible white glitter**

YOU WILL ALSO NEED
- ✳ **20cm round, non-stick loose-bottom cake tin**
- ✳ **reindeer or other Christmas cupcake toppers**

1 For the base, gently melt the butter, add the crushed digestives and mix well. Press into the base of the tin and chill to firm up.
2 For the filling, put the gelatine into cold water to soften, then dissolve it in 50ml water over a very gentle heat. Set aside to cool.
3 In a large bowl, beat the mascarpone, soft cheese and icing sugar until smooth, but be careful not to over-mix. Stir through the gelatine mixture, nuts and nougat pieces and vanilla until just combined. Spoon half the mixture into the tin and level to create a smooth top. Repeat with the remaining mixture and return to the fridge to set for at least 4 hrs or overnight.
4 To serve, decorate with shards of nougat or brittle, chopped pistachios, nougat pieces, a sprinkle of glitter and your choice of festive cupcake toppers.
Per serving: Cals 559, Fat 48g, Sat fat 29g, Carbs 24g

TIP
This is a lovely slightly soft-set cheesecake but if you prefer a firmer set (probably a good idea if you're on bring-a-pud duty and have to transport it), just add 2 more gelatine leaves

TIP
These are quite boozy – if you'd like a non-alcoholic version use Shloer rosé sparkling grape juice instead of Prosecco

Pink Prosecco jellies

A pretty, fun finale to any meal and it's low fat too!

Serves 8 • Ready in 20 mins, plus chilling

✳ **300 g | 10.5 oz caster sugar**
✳ **½tsp vanilla extract**
✳ **10 sheets leaf gelatine**
✳ **750 ml | 26 fl oz bottle pink Prosecco, chilled**
✳ **½tsp edible glitter**

1 Put the caster sugar in a pan with 250ml water. Heat gently, stirring, until dissolved. Bring to the boil and bubble for 2 mins. Remove from the heat, add the vanilla extract and leave to cool for 5 mins.
2 Soak the gelatine leaves in cold water for 3 mins to soften. Squeeze out the excess water then add to the warm syrup and stir until dissolved.
3 Pour in the Prosecco and edible glitter and stir to combine. Pour into 8 glasses and chill for about 5 hrs until set.
Per serving: Cals 238, Fat 0g, Sat fat 0g, Carbs 42g

Boozy fruits of the forest with white chocolate sauce

A 10-min pud you can satisfyingly put together at the last minute.

Serves 6 • Ready in 10 mins

* **500 g | 17 oz frozen fruits of the forest**
* **3tbsp black cherry jam**
* **3tbsp fruit-flavoured liqueur**
* **100 g | 3.5 oz white chocolate,** broken into squares
* **75 ml | 2.6 fl oz single cream**
* **500 ml | 17 fl oz good-quality vanilla ice cream**

1 Warm the frozen fruits and jam gently together in a pan until the fruits have just defrosted. Add the fruit liqueur and heat gently for a further 1 min.

2 Microwave the chocolate and cream together in a bowl on a very low setting for a few mins until melted. Stir until smooth.

3 To serve, spoon the warm fruit into 6 bowls or glasses, add a few spoonfuls of the hot white chocolate sauce and top with a scoop of vanilla ice cream.

Per serving: Cals 250, Fat 11g, Sat fat 7g, Carbs 30g

Christmas baked Alaska bombe

A showstopping alternative to a traditional pudding.

Serves 10 • Ready in 45 mins, plus soaking and freezing

- ✱ **200 g | 7 oz mixed dried fruit**
- ✱ **4tbsp brandy or dark rum**
- ✱ **400 g | 14 oz brioche loaf, crusts removed and cut into 1cm thick slices**
- ✱ **750 ml | 26 fl oz chocolate ice cream**
- ✱ **4 egg whites**
- ✱ **180 g | 6.5 fl oz caster sugar**
- ✱ **1½tsp cornflour**
- ✱ **1tsp white wine vinegar**

YOU WILL ALSO NEED
- ✱ **900 g | 2 lb pudding basin, lined with clingfilm**
- ✱ **indoor sparklers, to decorate (optional)**

1 Mix the fruit and alcohol in a food container and leave to soak overnight. Line the pudding basin tightly with brioche slices, reserving some to cover the filling.

2 Mash the ice cream with the soaked fruit until evenly mixed then spoon into the brioche-lined bowl, pressing down firmly and evenly. Cover with a layer of brioche, cover with clingfilm and freeze for at least 4 hrs, or it can be frozen for up to 1 month.

3 When ready to serve, heat the oven to 240°C/475°F/Gas Mark 9. Whisk the egg whites until stiff, gradually add the sugar, 1tbsp at a time, whisking well between each addition, until glossy and stiffly peaking. Whisk in the cornflour and vinegar.

4 Unwrap the ice-cream bombe and put on an ovenproof plate. Spoon the meringue all over to completely cover the bombe and swirl with the back of a spoon. Put the plate on a baking tray and bake for 5-8 mins until the meringue is golden. Decorate with indoor sparklers if using and serve straightaway.
Per serving: Cals 371, Fat 10g, Sat fat 6g, Carbs 61g

Raspberry macaron trifle

An easy cheat's dessert that looks and tastes amazing.

Serves 8 • Ready in 15 mins

- ✱ **24 sponge fingers**
- ✱ **150 ml | 5.3 fl oz muscat dessert wine (we used Brown Brothers Orange Muscat & Flora)**
- ✱ **450 g | 2.5 oz raspberries**
- ✱ **2 x 500 g | 17 oz tubs fresh vanilla custard**
- ✱ **300 ml | 10.5 fl oz half-fat double cream**
- ✱ **1tsp vanilla extract**
- ✱ **1tsp caster sugar**
- ✱ **12 pink macarons**

1 Arrange half the sponge fingers in the base of a deep trifle dish and drizzle over 75ml of the muscat wine.
2 Scatter over 175g of the raspberries and pour over the vanilla custard.
3 Cover with another layer of sponge fingers, drizzle over the remaining muscat and top with another 175g raspberries.
4 Whip the cream with the vanilla and caster sugar until softly peaking.
5 Arrange the macarons around the edge of the dish and pile the remaining raspberries in the centre.
Per serving: Cals 567, Fat 30g, Sat fat 18g, Carbs 59g

TIP
If you're not keen on dried fruits, make a mint chocolate bombe by stirring chopped After Eights or Matchmakers into the ice cream

Chocolate orange trifle

Buy easy-peel clementines and ask little hands to help peeling! If they want to eat it, too, swap the booze for orange juice.

Serves 10 · Ready in 25 mins, plus cooling

* 450 ml | 15.8 fl oz full-fat milk
* 1 vanilla pod, split and seed removed
* 3 medium eggs, plus 2 yolks
* 50 g | 1.7 oz caster sugar
* 4tsp cornflour
* 500 g | 17 oz chocolate chip brioche, sliced 1cm thick
* 4tbsp Cointreau or Triple Sec
* 700 g | 24 oz clementines, peeled and soaked in liqueur, then sliced into rounds (reserve 4tbsp liqueur)
* 600 ml | 21 fl oz double cream
* 4tbsp icing sugar
* Zest of 1 orange, to decorate
* Chocolate curls, to decorate

1 Heat the milk and vanilla seed until you see steam coming off the surface. Remove from heat and set aside. Whisk the eggs, yolks, sugar and cornflour together. Gradually whisk the milk into the egg mixture. Pour back into the pan and cook over a gentle heat, whisking constantly until thicker and smooth. Strain and leave to cool with a layer of clingfilm pressed onto the top to prevent a skin forming.
2 Lay the brioche slices on a plate and drizzle over the Cointreau. Put half the slices in the base of a deep 3-litre trifle bowl and scatter over half the clementine rounds before pouring over half the cooled custard.
3 Whip the cream, icing sugar and reserved liqueur until it forms loose peaks; spoon half onto the fruit. Scatter with remaining brioche, fruit and custard, then top with remaining cream. Sprinkle over the zest and chocolate curls. Chill until ready to serve.
Per serving: Cals 641, Fat 43g, Sat Fat 25g, Carbs 49g

TIP
Add the vanilla pod to a jar of sugar for your own homemade vanilla sugar, great for baking!

Chocolate and chestnut roulade with cream liqueur

This decadent log is the perfect dessert for a celebratory dinner.

Serves 10 • Ready in 40 mins, plus resting

* **175 g | 6 oz dark chocolate**
* **6 large organic eggs, separated**
* **175 g | 6 oz caster sugar (plus 1tbsp)**

FOR THE FILLING

* **145 ml | 5 fl oz whipping cream**
* **250 g | 8.8 oz can sweetened chestnut purée**
* **2tbsp cream liqueur (we Coole Swan Superior Dairy Cream)**
* **Marrons glacés, to decorate**

1 Preheat the oven to 180°C/350°F/ Gas Mark 4. Grease and line a 22cm by 33cm Swiss roll tin. Melt the chocolate in a bowl over a pan of simmering water. Place the egg yolks and 175g sugar into a large bowl and whisk for 5 mins, until pale, thick and creamy. Whisk in the melted chocolate.

2 In a clean bowl, whisk the egg whites until they form stiff peaks. Fold 1tbsp of the egg white into the chocolate mix to loosen. Gently fold in the remainder, then pour into the prepared tin and level. Bake for about 20 mins until spongy to the touch.

3 Sprinkle a sheet of baking paper with 1tbsp caster sugar. Cool the roulade for a few mins in the tin then turn out on to the sugared paper and peel off the backing paper. Cover with a clean sheet of baking paper and a damp tea towel and leave for 1 hour.

4 To make the filling, whip the cream until it forms soft peaks. Fold in the chestnut purée and liqueur and spread over the roulade. Roll up from one short end, using the sugared paper to help you. Serve with marrons glacés, if liked.

Per serving: Cals 318, Fat 15.5g, Sat Fat 8g, Carbs 37g

TIP
Add 3tbsp of your fave festive tipple for a grown-up version of this crowd pleaser

Mulled berry snowflake tart

Pull out all the stops and wow your friends with this show-stopping tart.

Serves 6 • Ready in 1 hr 40 mins

* **375 g | 13 oz sheet of shortcrust pastry**
* **4tbsp apple juice**
* **2tbsp port**
* **175 g | 6 oz caster sugar, plus extra for snowflake frosting**
* **1tsp ground cinnamon**
* **A grating of fresh nutmeg**
* **300 g | 10.5 oz fresh or frozen cranberries**
* **2tbsp cornflour mixed with 1½tbsp cold water**
* **300 g | 10.5 frozen mixed berries**
* **Icing sugar, to dust**

1 Line a 26 x 19cm fluted tart tin with the pastry and trim off the excess. Re-roll out the pastry trimmings and, using snowflake cutters, cut out 15 snowflakes of various sizes. Put the tart tin and pastry snowflakes in the fridge to chill while you make the filling.
2 Heat the apple juice and port with the sugar in a pan until dissolved. Stir in the spices and cranberries and heat for 1 min, or a little longer if using frozen fruit. Remove from the heat and stir in the cornflour paste. Heat for 2-3 mins until thickened slightly, add the remaining fruit, heat for a further 1 min, and then set aside to cool.
3 Heat the oven to 200°C/400°F/Gas Mark 6. Line the pastry with foil, fill with baking beans and bake for 15 mins. Remove the foil and beans and cook for a further 5 mins. Turn the oven down to 180°C/350°F/Gas Mark 4. Pour the fruit filling into the tin and bake for 35 mins.
4 While the tart is cooking, put a little caster sugar on to a plate and dip the pastry snowflakes on one side. Put the snowflakes on a baking tray, sugar-side up, and bake in the oven with the tart for 15 mins. Lay the snowflakes over the tart and dust with icing sugar.
Per serving: Cals 464, Fat 20g, Sat Fat 7g, Carbs 63g

Panettone pudding

This recipe is perfect to use up any leftover panettone, if there is such a thing!

Serves 10 • Ready in 1 hr

* **100 g | 3.5 oz sultanas**
* **100 ml | 3.5 fl oz strong black tea**
* **75 g | 2.6 oz butter, softened, plus extra for greasing**
* **1 x 500 g | 17 oz panettone, sliced**
* **3 large eggs**
* **250 ml | 8.8 fl oz whole milk**
* **150 ml | 5.3 fl oz double cream**
* **25 g | 0.8 oz caster sugar**
* **25 g | 0.8 oz demerara sugar**
* **Single cream or custard, to serve**

1 Put the sultanas into a small pan with the tea. Heat gently, then set aside to allow the fruit to soak up the tea. Heat the oven to 180°C/ 350°F/ Gas Mark 4.
2 Grease a 2-litre baking dish. Butter the panettone slices and cut into triangles. Arrange the triangles so that they sit a bit upright and overlap in the dish, then scatter over the drained sultanas between the layers.
3 Lightly beat the eggs and mix with the milk, cream and caster sugar, then pour over the panettone. Lightly press down, so that the bread absorbs the creamy mixture. Leave for 30 mins (or leave in the fridge overnight).
4 Sprinkle over the demerara sugar and bake for 30 mins (or leave it a little longer if cooking after chilling overnight) until the top is golden and the pudding is just set. Serve warm with single cream or custard.
Per serving: Cals 414, Fat 26g, Sat Fat 15g, Carbs 36g

TIP
Add some sparkle by decorating the pastry snowflakes with silver sprinkles and edible glitter spray

TIP
Freeze the marquise, sauce & plums separately. Defrost overnight in the fridge

Chocolate marquise with sugar plum butterscotch sauce

Chocolate, fruit and butterscotch, what's not to love?

Serves 12 • Ready in 40 mins, plus chilling

* ✳ **12 plums, stoned and quartered**
* **FOR THE MARQUISE**
* ✳ **300 g ǀ 10.5 oz dark chocolate, finely chopped**
* ✳ **125 g ǀ 4.4 oz unsalted butter, cubed**
* ✳ **6 large egg yolks**
* ✳ **150 g ǀ 5.3 oz golden caster sugar**
* ✳ **500ml ǀ 17 fl oz double cream**
* ✳ **45 g ǀ 1.5 oz cocoa powder, sifted**
* **FOR THE SAUCE**
* ✳ **45 g ǀ 1.5 oz golden syrup**
* ✳ **75 g ǀ 2.6 oz light muscovado sugar**
* ✳ **30 g ǀ 1 oz butter**
* ✳ **75 ml ǀ 2.6 fl oz double cream**
* ✳ **1tsp vanilla extract**
* ✳ **1.5 litre terrine**

1 To make the marquise, melt the chocolate and butter in a heavy-based pan over a low heat. Mix well then set aside to cool. Using a mixer, beat the egg yolks with the sugar, until creamy and thick.
2 Turn the speed to low and, while continuing to mix, pour in the chocolate in a slow, steady stream. Still on a low speed, add half the cream and mix until well incorporated. Add the cocoa, a heaped tbsp at a time. Mix in the rest of the cream, being careful not to over mix.
3 Double-line the terrine with cling film, leaving excess over the sides. Spoon the mixture into the tin and smooth the surface. Leave in the fridge to set for 3 hrs or overnight. Turn out on to a serving plate and

use a dry palette knife to smooth rough edges.
4 Put the plums in a pan with 1tbsp of water, cover and heat gently for around 4 mins, or until they're softened and juicy. Set aside to cool.
5 To make the sauce, put the syrup, sugar and butter in a pan and heat gently, until sugar has dissolved. Turn up the heat and bubble gently for 5 mins. Slowly pour in the cream and vanilla. Stir well. Remove from the heat to cool.
6 Spoon the plums and their juice over the marquise and finish with a drizzle of butterscotch sauce.
Per serving: Cals 608, Fat 42g, Sat Fat 28g, Carbs 41g

Creamy baked rice pudding

Love it or hate it, you can't deny this rice pudding looks delicious!

Serves 4 • Ready in 2 hrs

* ✳ **175 ml ǀ 6 oz short-grain rice**
* ✳ **100 g ǀ 3.5 oz golden caster sugar**
* ✳ **410 g ǀ 7 oz can evaporated milk**
* ✳ **900 ml ǀ 32 fl oz Jersey milk**
* ✳ **½-1 whole nutmeg, grated**
* ✳ **30 g ǀ 1 oz butter, diced**
* ✳ **1.5 litre ovenproof dish, buttered**

1 Heat the oven to 150°C/ 300°F/Gas Mark 2. Sprinkle the rice and sugar into the prepared dish. Pour over the evaporated milk and Jersey milk. Sprinkle surface with nutmeg, according to taste, and dot with butter.
2 Put dish on a tray in the oven. Bake for 45 mins, stir and then bake for 1 hour 30 mins more. It's ready when the rice grains have plumped up, the milk has thickened and there's a lovely skin.
3 Ways to serve: Use a can of coconut milk instead of evaporated milk and serve with a sprinkling of coconut chips.
4 Top with slivers of stem ginger in syrup.
5 Serve with dollops of blackberry and apple compote.
Per serving: Cals 648, Fat 27g, Sat Fat 17g, Carbs 81g

TIP
No need to specially buy short-grain rice if you have Italian Arborio risotto rice. Use that, as it gives an even creamier result

The Day
AFTER

Easy ideas for
LEFTOVERS

Turn your Christmas dinner leftovers into
delicious next-day dishes

TIP
If you don't have any leftover greens, use any type of cabbage, lightly steaming it first

Bubble and squeak

This is the ultimate Boxing Day brunch dish. Serve with your favourite sausages, crispy bacon or a soft-poached egg.

Serves 4 • Ready in 20 mins

* **800 g | 1.7 lb leftover roast or mashed potatoes**
* **A little milk, cream or crème fraîche (optional)**
* **50 g | 1.7 oz butter**
* **1 large onion, chopped**
* **400 g | 14 oz leftover green vegetables, roughly chopped**
* **3tbsp capers**
* **2tbsp vegetable oil**

1 If using roast potatoes, mash roughly in a large bowl, adding a couple of tablespoons of milk, cream or crème fraîche if they're a little dry.
2 Melt half the butter in a frying pan and gently cook the onion for 10 mins until soft. Tip into the mash along with the greens and capers, season well and mix together.
3 Wipe the frying pan with kitchen paper, then add the remaining butter and the vegetable oil and return to the heat. Take large spoonfuls of the potato mixture and space them out in the pan, patting them down into flat cakes.
4 Fry gently for about 2 mins on each side until golden. Repeat with any remaining mixture.
Per serving: Cals 531, Fat 28g, Sat fat 8g, Carbs 56g

Cheese and cranberry toasties

Who doesn't love a toastie? These sandwiches combine cranberries with salty Parma ham and Cheddar for the perfect balance.

Serves 4 • Ready in 15 mins

* **200 g | 7 oz Cheddar cheese, grated**
* **1 x 80 g | 2.8 oz pack Parma ham**
* **2tbsp cranberry sauce**
* **8 slices good-quality sourdough bread**
* **50 g | 1.7 oz butter**

1 Bring a large heavy-bottomed frying pan to a medium heat.
2 Divide the cheese, Parma ham and cranberry sauce between 4 slices of bread. Top with the remaining bread and press down firmly. Spread the outside of each side of the toasties with the butter.
3 Fry the toasties gently for 3-5 mins on each side, pushing down with a fish slice until the cheese is melted and the outside is golden. Remove, slice and serve.
Per serving: Cals 605, Fat 32g, Sat fat 18g, Carbs 49g

TIP
Can't find fresh apricots? Use half the quantity of dried, soaked in hot water to soften

Fragrant turkey curry

TIP
You can use ready-made stock and leftover ham instead of starting from scratch

Roast ham, pea and mint stew

Fragrant turkey curry

A real Christmas leftovers classic, turkey is transformed in a mild, sweet curry sauce with just a handful of other ingredients.

Serves 4 • Ready in 35 mins

* 50 g | 1.7 oz butter or ghee
* 2 onions, sliced
* 3 garlic cloves, thinly sliced
* 2 x thumb-sized pieces ginger, grated
* 4tbsp curry powder
* 6 cardamom pods, lightly bashed
* 100 g | 3.5 oz apricots, roughly chopped
* 200 ml | 7 fl oz chicken stock
* 1tbsp mango chutney
* 400 g | 14 oz fresh tomatoes, diced
* 400 g | 14 oz leftover cooked turkey, shredded
* steamed white rice, to serve
* handful toasted flaked almonds, to garnish
* coriander, to garnish

1 Add the butter or ghee to a large pan, over a medium heat. Mix in the onion and cook for 5 mins until soft and starting to become translucent. Add the garlic and ginger and cook gently for a further 3-4 mins. Add the curry powder and cardamom and cook for 2 mins more.
2 Stir through the apricots, chicken stock, mango chutney and tomatoes. Leave to bubble for 15 mins, until the sauce has thickened. Check and adjust seasoning to taste.
3 Add the turkey and cook for 5 mins until heated through. Serve with steamed white rice, topped with a scattering of flaked almonds and a handful of coriander.
Per serving: Cals 400, Fat 14g, Sat fat, 7g, Carbs 5g

Roast ham, pea and mint stew

A deliciously flavourful winter warmer, ideal for a cosy night in.

Serves 4 • Ready in 2 hrs 25 mins

* 850 g | 1.8 lb whole ham, skin removed
* 500 ml | 17 fl oz medium dry cider
* 1½tbsp runny honey
* 1½tbsp wholegrain mustard
* 25 g | 0.8 oz butter
* 1 onion, sliced
* 500 g | 17 oz baby new potatoes
* 1 bay leaf
* 2 sprigs thyme
* 250 g | 8.8 oz frozen peas
* small handful each of mint and flat-leaf parsley leaves, finely chopped

1 Heat the oven to 180°C/350°F/Gas Mark 4. Put the ham in a pan that it just fits, cover with cold water, bring to the boil and then discard the water. Return the ham to the pan and pour in the cider, topping up with enough water to just cover. Bring to the boil and simmer for 1 hr 15 mins. Take out the ham and reserve the stock.
2 Partially cut the ham away from the bone, so the surface area is flattened out. Mix the honey and mustard and rub all over the meat. Put in a roasting tin and cook for 30 mins.
3 Meanwhile, melt the butter in a large pan, add the onion and cook gently for 5 mins, then stir in the potatoes, bay and thyme. Season with pepper. Cover with 700ml of the ham stock, bring to the boil and simmer gently for 15-20 mins. Roughly tear the ham off the bone and add to the stew with the peas.
4 Cook for 1 min, then lightly mash a third of the veg in the pan to slightly thicken the stew. Stir in the herbs just before serving.
Per serving: Cals 385, Fat 12g, Sat fat, 5g, Carbs 24g

Turkey, ham and chestnut pie

Here's another satisfying way of using up festive leftovers.

Serves 4 • Ready in 1 hr 20 mins

* 50 g | 1.7 oz butter, plus extra for greasing
* 450 g | 15.8 oz leeks, trimmed and cut into 1cm-thick slices
* 2tsp thyme leaves
* 50 g | 1.7 oz plain flour
* 500 ml | 17 fl oz turkey stock
* 300 g | 10.5 oz cooked turkey, cut into large pieces
* 200 g | 7 oz cooked ham, cut into cubes
* 100 g | 3.5 oz cooked chestnuts, quartered
* 75 g | 2.6 oz crème fraîche
* grating of fresh nutmeg
* 350 g | 12.3 oz ready-made puff pastry
* 1 egg yolk, beaten

YOU WILL ALSO NEED
* 30.5 x 25.5cm pie dish

1 Melt the butter in a large pan or casserole dish, add the leeks and thyme, then stir, cover and cook gently for 15 mins until soft. Add the flour and stir well. Pour in the stock, stirring, until you have a smooth sauce. Add the meats, chestnuts and crème fraîche, and season with black pepper, a little nutmeg and salt, if needed. Stir well to combine.
2 Put the filling into the pie dish. Heat the oven to 200°C/400°F/Gas Mark 6. Butter the rim of the dish. Roll the pastry out to the thickness of a £1 coin, cut several strips and press them around the edges of the dish. Brush with water and lie a pastry lid on top. Make 2 small steam holes.
3 Press the pastry edges together, trim off any excess, then crimp the edges. Use excess to decorate the top. Mix the egg yolk with 1tsp water and brush all over the pastry.
4 Place the dish on a baking tray and bake for 30-35 mins, or until the pastry is brown and the filling piping hot. Serve immediately.
Per serving: Cals 802, Fat 44g, Sat fat 24g, Carbs 51g

This wonderfully comforting pie has all the flavours of Christmas topped off with a flaky puff-pastry lid

TIP
Instead of pastry, you could cook some dumplings on top of the stew at the end of step one

Stuffing and root veg hash

Using leftovers makes this recipe super quick to produce.

Serves 4 • Ready in 20 mins

✳ **500 g | 17 oz roasted root veg (potatoes, carrots, parsnips), mashed**
✳ **300 g | 10.5 oz leftover cooked veg (sliced sprouts, peas, cabbage), mashed**
✳ **400 g | 14 oz leftover cooked stuffing or sausages, roughly chopped**
✳ **2tsp fresh thyme, leaves picked**
✳ **zest of 1 lemon**
✳ **½tsp smoked paprika**
✳ **pinch of chilli flakes**
✳ **2 eggs, beaten, plus 4 to serve**
✳ **3tbsp olive oil**
✳ **6 vine tomatoes, halved**

1 Heat the grill to high. Mix together all the veg with the stuffing, thyme, lemon zest, paprika, chilli flakes and beaten egg. Season well.
2 Heat 2tbsp oil in a large frying pan and fry the hash for 5 mins until golden. Flip over and fry for another 5 mins.
3 In another frying pan, fry the 4 eggs in the remaining oil and grill the tomatoes for 10 mins. Serve the hash with the fried eggs on top and the grilled tomatoes on the side.
Per serving: Cals 813, Fat 45g, Sat fat 10.5g, Carbs 23g

TIP
To flip the hash, cover with a large plate and carefully turn over, then slide back into the pan

TIP
If your Christmas gammon has already been devoured, just fry off some pancetta

Melty baked fondue cheese

Create the ultimate sharing dish!
Serve 4 • Ready in 20 mins

* **200 g | 7 oz Brie or Camembert, rind removed**
* **125 g | 4.4 oz Gruyère cheese**
* **100 g | 3.5 oz cream cheese**
* **3tbsp milk or white wine**
* **2tbsp Parmesan cheese, grated**
* **2tsp cornflour**
* **5tbsp chutney**
* **1tsp thyme sprigs**
* **bread, to serve**

1 Heat the oven to 170°C/325°F/Gas Mark 3. Put the cheeses and cream cheese into a processor with milk or wine, half the Parmesan and cornflour. Blend until smooth. Spoon the chutney into the base of an ovenproof dish and spoon on the creamy cheese. Season well, sprinkle with thyme and the remaining Parmesan.
2 Bake for 20 mins until pale golden. Serve with bread.
Per serving: Cals 449, Fat 33g, Sat fat 21g, Carbs 12g

TIP
If you love strong blue cheese, crumble in some Stilton, too

Quick gammon and pea carbonara

Here's a delicious twist on a classic. This speedy pasta recipe makes a lovely change as a way of using up any remaining ham.

Serves 4 • Ready in 20 mins

* **450 g | 16 oz leftover gammon, shredded**
* **6 egg yolks**
* **100 g | 3.5 oz Parmesan cheese, finely grated, plus some for serving**
* **400 g | 14 oz spaghetti**
* **100 g | 3.5 oz frozen peas**

1 Over a medium heat in a heavy-bottomed frying pan, reheat the gammon for a few mins until starting to crisp.
2 Meanwhile, whisk the egg yolks thoroughly with the Parmesan cheese and plenty of black pepper.
3 Cook the spaghetti, according to packet instructions, adding the peas to the boiling water 3 mins before the end. Drain the peas and pasta, reserving some of the cooking liquid.
4 Return the pasta and peas to the pan and very quickly stir through the gammon, egg and Parmesan mixture, adding the reserved cooking liquid a little at a time until you have your preferred consistency and a glossy finish.
Per serving: Cals 847, Fat 38g, Sat fat 15g, Carbs 75g

TIP
For that extra touch of luxury, add a splash of truffle oil to the mix

Ham hock mac and cheese

TIP
You can also use leftover cooked salmon, broken into chunky flakes

Smoked salmon and potato crustless quiche

Ham hock mac and cheese

A great crowd-pleaser, this is super-easy to prepare.

Serves 8 • Ready in 1 hr

* 375 g | 13 oz macaroni or casarecce pasta
* 125 g | 4.4 oz butter
* 100 g | 3.5 oz plain flour
* 1 litre milk
* 2tbsp Dijon mustard
* 300 g | 10.5 oz Gruyère, grated
* 150 g | 5.3 oz extra-mature Cheddar, grated
* 500 g | 17 oz ham hock, shredded
* 100 g | 3.5 oz fresh breadcrumbs

1 Cook the pasta in a large pan of boiling salted water until just tender. Drain and toss in olive oil to prevent sticking.
2 Melt the butter in a large pan, stir in the flour and cook out for a few mins. Heat the milk separately, then whisk into the flour and butter over a low heat until thickened. Stir in the mustard and all the cheese, reserving 5tbsp.
3 Heat the oven to 190°C/375°F/Gas Mark 5. Mix the sauce into the pasta and add the ham. Put into a large gratin dish and top with the breadcrumbs and reserved cheese.
4 Bake for 35 mins until piping hot, golden brown and bubbling.
Per serving: Cals 777, Fat 41g, Sat fat 24g, Carbs 59g

Smoked salmon and potato crustless quiche

No faffing about with pastry here – just layer in a tin and bake.

Serves 6 • Ready in 1 hr

* 750 g | 1.6 lb new potatoes, cooked
* 200 g | 7 oz smoked salmon, cut into strips
* 6 spring onions, sliced
* 2tbsp chopped fresh dill
* 4 eggs
* 200 ml | 7 fl oz crème fraîche

YOU WILL ALSO NEED
* 18 x 28cm traybake tin, lined with baking paper

1 Heat the oven to 180°C/350°F/Gas Mark 4. Slice the potatoes and arrange half of them over the base of the lined tin. Season with salt and pepper.
2 Arrange half the smoked salmon pieces over the potatoes and scatter over half of the spring onions and half of the dill. Repeat the layers with the remaining potatoes, salmon, spring onions and dill.
3 Beat together the eggs and crème fraîche and pour over the layered veg and salmon. Bake for 45-50 mins until just set in the centre. If the top starts to over-brown during cooking, cover with a sheet of baking paper. Serve warm or cold.
Per serving: Cals 335, Fat 20g, Sat fat 11g, Carbs 21g

Cheeseboard fondue

This one may be a bit naughty – but it is Christmas, after all!

Serves 8 • Ready in 15 mins

* 300 ml | 10.5 fl oz pale ale
* 2 garlic cloves, finely chopped few sprigs rosemary
* 950 g | 2.1 lb leftover cheese, grated (we like a mix of hard and soft)
* a selection of steamed potatoes, crunchy vegetables, stale bread cubes, pickles and charcuterie meats, to serve

1 Add the ale, garlic and rosemary to a large pan and simmer for a few mins. Stir through the cheese, a little at a time, mixing thoroughly before each new addition.
2 Once everything is melted, serve it immediately, keeping it warm if possible over a fondue ring or tealight. Serve with your chosen sides, and let everyone dunk their own meat, veggies or bread for a fun, sharing meal.
Per serving: Cals 570, Fat 43g, Sat fat 27g, Carbs 11g

Choose one of these relaxed, no-fuss recipes for when you want to produce a pleasing meal with minimum effort

TIP
This couldn't be quicker or easier to whip up for unexpected visitors

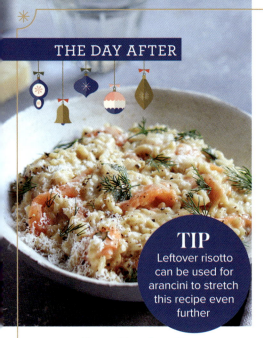

TIP
Leftover risotto can be used for arancini to stretch this recipe even further

Smoked salmon risotto

Rich and indulgent, this simple risotto is finished with cream and butter for a silky-smooth texture.

Serves 4 • Ready in 40 mins

* 2tbsp extra-virgin olive oil
* 1 onion, finely diced
* 240 g | 8.4 oz carnaroli rice
* 1 litre fish or shellfish stock
* 2tbsp butter
* 2tbsp double cream
* 100 g | 3.5 oz Parmesan cheese, grated
* 120 g | 4.3 oz smoked salmon
* dill, to serve (optional)

1 Add the oil and onion to a large pan. Bring to a medium heat and cook the onions for 10 mins, until soft and translucent. Stir through the rice, and mix for 2 mins more to toast the rice.
2 Add the stock and simmer for 20-25 mins, stirring regularly. If the rice has absorbed all of the liquid before it's cooked through, add a little more stock.
3 Remove from the heat and stir through the butter, cream and cheese. Mix through the smoked salmon and top with the dill, if using.
Per serving: Cals 538, Fat 27g, Sat fat 13g, Carbs 52g

Brie and cranberry quiche

Filling, gooey and simply delicious.

Serves 6 • Ready in 1 hr, plus chilling

FOR THE PASTRY
* 200 g | 7 oz plain flour
* 100 g | 3.5 oz chilled butter, cubed
* 1 egg

FOR THE FILLING
* 30 g | 1 oz butter
* 1 large onion, chopped
* 250 g | 8.8 oz streaky bacon, chopped
* 5 eggs, lightly beaten
* 400 ml | 7 fl oz crème fraîche
* 125 g | 4.4 oz Brie, sliced
* 3tbsp cranberry sauce
* 60 g | 2 oz Cheddar cheese, grated

YOU WILL ALSO NEED
* 20cm loose-based tart tin, greased

1 For the pastry, put the flour, butter and a pinch of salt into a food processor. Whizz until the mixture resembles crumbs, then add the egg and 1tbsp cold water. Blend until just bound. Turn out onto a lightly floured work surface and knead until smooth. Wrap in clingfilm and chill for 30 mins.
2 Roll out the pastry and use to line the tin. Chill for 20 mins. Put a baking tray into oven and heat to 200°C/ 400°F/ Gas Mark 6. Trim the pastry case and bake blind directly on the baking tray for 10 mins, then remove the paper and baking beans and cook for 10 mins more.
3 Heat the butter and fry the onions gently for 5 mins to soften. Put the bacon in another pan, cover with cold water and bring to the boil. Drain, pat dry and add to the onions to crisp.
4 Crack the eggs into a jug, add the crème fraîche, season and whisk. Spoon the onions and bacon into the pastry case. Arrange the Brie on top with teaspoonfuls of cranberry sauce. Scatter over the Cheddar, and pour egg mixture over. Bake for 30 mins until golden and firm. Serve warm.
Per serving: Cals 854, Fat 67g, Sat fat 40g, Carbs 32g

TIP
Smoked salmon would make a tasty alternative to bacon

TIP
Replace the turkey with prawns or extra veg, depending on what you have to hand

Thai-style turkey and noodle soup

Craving something healthy? This spicy soup is just the ticket!

Serves 4 • Ready in 20 mins

- ✳ 125 g | 4.4 oz Thai rice noodles
- ✳ 2tbsp Thai red curry paste
- ✳ 2 x 400 ml | 14 fl oz cans coconut milk
- ✳ 200 g | 7 oz cooked leftover turkey, broken into pieces
- ✳ 1 bunch spring onions, sliced
- ✳ 1 red pepper, deseeded and sliced
- ✳ finely grated zest and juice of 1 lime
- ✳ dash of fish sauce
- ✳ pinch of sugar
- ✳ fresh coriander, for garnish

1 Put noodles into a large bowl and pour over enough boiling water to cover. Leave for 4 mins or until noodles have softened.

2 Meanwhile, put Thai red curry paste into a pan with coconut milk. Heat gently, stirring. Add turkey, spring onions, pepper, lime zest and juice, fish sauce and sugar. Warm through for a few mins.
3 Drain and add noodles to the soup. Heat for 1 min, then garnish with coriander to serve.
Per serving: Cals 255, Fat 5.5g, Sat fat 2g, Carbs 22g

149

Christmas pudding cranachan

This traditional Scottish dessert is an absolutely excellent way to make excess Christmas pudding go further.

Makes 4 · Ready in 10 mins, plus cooling

* 75 g | 2.6 oz pinhead oats
* 50 g | 1.7 oz soft, light brown sugar
* 260 ml | 8.9 fl oz double cream
* 1tsp honey
* 2tbsp whisky
* 100 g | 3.5 oz leftover Christmas pudding, crumbled
* 120 g | 4.2 oz berry compote
* 100 g | 3.5 oz fresh raspberries, halved
* chopped nuts, to serve

1 Bring a heavy-bottomed pan to a high heat; add the oats and brown sugar and toast until golden. Tip the mixture out onto a baking tray and leave to cool.

2 Whip together the cream, honey and whisky to soft peaks.

3 In individual glasses, layer up the oats, whisky cream, Christmas pudding, compote and raspberries. Keep chilled until ready to eat, then sprinkle with chopped nuts just before serving.

Per serving: Cals 555, Fat 38g, Sat fat 23g, Carbs 42g

TIP
You can make this ahead of time if you have room in your fridge

TIP
Keep the dough in the freezer and simply cut and bake whenever you have a cookie craving

Selection-box choc-chip cookies

Leftover nuts and selection box chocs both star in this simple cookie recipe, great for kids (big or little) to make. It only works if there *are* leftover chocs, of course!

Makes 30 • Ready in 25 mins

* ✳ 225 g | 8.2 oz salted butter, softened
* ✳ 75 g | 2.6 oz caster sugar
* ✳ 160 g | 5.8 oz light brown sugar
* ✳ 1tsp vanilla paste
* ✳ 2 eggs
* ✳ 350 g | 13 oz plain flour
* ✳ 350 g | 13 oz leftover selection box chocolates, roughly chopped
* ✳ 100 g | 3.5 oz mixed nuts

1 In an electric mixer, beat the butter, sugars and vanilla together until light and creamy, about 5 mins. Add the eggs one at a time and beat until combined. Add the flour and mix briefly to form a dough. Add the chopped chocolate, reserving a handful, and combine.
2 Roll the cookie dough into a 35cm-long sausage shape in clingfilm, Refrigerate until firm.
3 Meanwhile, heat the oven to 190°C/375°F/Gas Mark 5. Blitz the nuts in a food processor. Remove the cookie dough from the fridge and roll in the nuts. With a serrated knife, cut into 5mm-thick slices.
4 Put cookies on a lined baking tray and scatter over reserved chopped chocolate. Bake for 12 mins or until golden around the edges. Cool on a wire rack before serving.
Per serving: Cals 203, Fat 10g, Sat fat 5g, Carbs 25g

THE BEST-EVER
Buffet

Jalapeño salsa verde and pork potato salad

Much more exciting than the standard potato salad, this one comes with an aromatic tang.

Serves 8-10 • Ready in 25 mins

* **900 g | 31 oz baby potatoes**
FOR THE SALSA VERDE
* **5tbsp extra virgin olive oil**
* **2tbsp red wine vinegar**
* **1 garlic clove, crushed**
* **1tbsp capers**
* **2tsp Dijon mustard**
* **2 fresh jalapeño chillies, sliced or 2tbsp of jarred jalapeños**
* **25 g | 0.8 oz bunch basil**
* **25 g | 0.8 oz bunch mint**
* **25 g | 0.8 oz bunch parsley**
* **450 g | 15.8 oz leftover roast pork, pulled or cut into chunks (you can also use cooked and sliced pork chops)**
* **150 g | 5.3 oz soft Agen prunes, halved**
* **75 g | 2.6 oz rocket or watercress**

1 Pour cold water over the potatoes in a pan and season. Bring the potatoes to the boil, then simmer until tender. Drain and set aside.
2 To make the salsa verde, in a food processor, pulse the oil, vinegar, garlic, capers, mustard, half the jalapeños and the herbs to form a paste. Add a little water if it's too thick.
3 In a bowl, mix the potatoes with a few tablespoons of salsa verde. Warm the pork, then mix into the potatoes along with the prunes. Stir in the rocket or watercress. Top with the remaining jalapeños and drizzle over more dressing – serve the rest on the side.
Per serving: Cals 281-225, Fat 11-9g, Sat fat 2.5-2g, Carbs 24-19g

Chicken liver parfait

A few chicken livers go a long way. This ticks all the boxes – classic, tasty and great value for money.

Serves 6-8 • Ready in 45 mins, plus chilling

* **250 g | 8.8 oz unsalted butter, softened**
* **1 onion, peeled and finely chopped**
* **1 garlic clove, crushed**
* **400 g | 14 oz chicken livers**
* **2tbsp each port and brandy**
* **fresh bay leaves**
* **toast, to serve**
YOU WILL ALSO NEED
* **1 terrine dish or 6-8 mini ramekins**

1 First, clarify some butter. Gently melt half the butter then pour off the yellow butter, leaving the milky residue in the pan (which you can discard). Leave it to cool.
2 Add a little of the remaining butter to a frying pan and sauté the onion until soft. Add the garlic and fry for 1 min. Remove from the pan and set aside.
3 Prepare the livers by trimming off any discoloured areas and sinew. Season the livers with salt and cook in the pan for around 2 mins; brown them but they should be pink inside. Add the port and brandy, and bring to the boil for a minute.
4 Season, allow to cool slightly then whizz the livers in a food processor with the onion, garlic and remaining unclarified butter. Spoon into the terrine mould or ramekins, level the surface and top with fresh bay leaves.
5 Gently pour over the clarified butter then chill for at least 6 hrs. When ready, serve with toast. This parfait will keep in the fridge for 1 week – the clarified butter helps to preserve it, but you don't have to eat it!
Per serving: Cals 323-430, Fat 29-39g, Sat fat 18-24g, Carbs 5-7g

Duck and healthy greens salad

Think Chinese-style crispy duck with a punchy Asian dressing served with crunchy greens.

Serves 6 • Ready in 2 hrs 40 mins

FOR THE DUCK
* 4 duck legs
* 150 ml | 5.3 fl oz soy sauce
* ½ cm piece of root ginger, roughly chopped
* 4 garlic cloves, bruised
* 2 star anise
* 1 cinnamon stick

FOR THE SALAD
* 300 g | 10.5 oz tenderstem broccoli
* 300 g | 10.5 oz kale, shredded
* 4tbsp mixed seeds, lightly toasted

FOR THE DRESSING
* 2tbsp sweet miso paste
* 1tbsp toasted sesame oil
* juice of 2 limes
* 1tbsp runny honey

1 Heat the oven to 200°C/400°F/Gas Mark 6. Put the duck legs skin-side down in a deep pan and pour over the soy sauce and enough water to cover. Add the ginger, garlic, star anise and the cinnamon stick, cover with a lid and bring to the boil. Reduce the heat to a gentle simmer and cook for 30 mins.

2 Turn the duck legs over and continue poaching for 1-1½ hrs or until tender. Remove from the heat and set aside to cool, then remove from the cooking liquor and pat dry

3 Meanwhile, bring a pan of water to the boil, cook the broccoli for 2 mins then rinse in cold water and set aside. Put the kale in a large bowl, cover with boiling water and leave for 1 min. Drain and rinse under cold water, then set aside.

4 Put the duck legs in the oven, skin side up, for 20-30 mins, until crisp then shred while hot. Combine the dressing ingredients until smooth, then toss with the kale, broccoli, shredded duck and seeds.

It will keep, dressed, for 4 hrs.
Per serving: Cals 299, Fat 25g, Sat Fat 7.9g, Carbs 3.5g

Tear & share Christmas tree bread

Tear & share Christmas tree bread

A showstopping centrepiece for your festive buffet. Melt a Camembert in the oven for luxurious dipping.

Serves 12 • Ready in 1 hr 30 mins

* **2 x 500 g | 17 oz Ciabatta Bread Mix**
* **sprigs of thyme**
* **small bunch sage, leaves chopped**
* **125 g | 4.4 oz packet butter with crushed garlic (we used Lurpak)**
* **8tbsp olive oil**
* **sea salt**

1 Tip the bread mix into a large bowl or the bowl of a freestanding mixer, fitted with a dough hook.
2 Add 1tbsp thyme leaves and 1tbsp chopped sage leaves. Pour in 4tbsp oil and add almost all from 600ml lukewarm water. Bring the mixture together to make a sticky dough.
3 Knead by hand, or in the mixer with the dough hook, for 5 mins, until smooth and silky. Cover and leave for 5 mins.
4 Tip the dough onto a floured surface and knead lightly, to make a smooth dough. Divide into 25, then roll into balls, flatten slightly and put a small knob of garlic butter in each then gather up the edges of the dough to cover the butter.
5 Arrange the rolls in a triangular shape on the baking tray to form the outside of the tree, then arrange the remaining dough balls in the centre, positioning 2 at the base in the centre to simulate a pot.
6 Cover with a clean, greased plastic bag and leave until doubled in size – roughly 20 mins.
7 Heat the oven to 220°C/425°F/ Gas Mark 7. Remove the bag and bake the bread for 30 mins. Scatter over a few more thyme and sage leaves and drizzle with oil, turning as needed until evenly golden brown.
8 Cook for 5 mins more, or longer if necessary, until base is really firm. Cover any areas that are browning quicker than others with foil. Scatter with sea salt.
9 If preparing ahead, warm in the oven at 180°C/350°F/Gas Mark 4 for 10 mins to serve.
Per serving: Cals 169, Fat 4.9g, Sat fat 4.8g, Carbs 27g

Jolly red salad

Another delicious side that won't wilt in minutes and will give weary palates a welcome boost of crisp and crunch.

Serves 6 • Ready in 30 mins

* **¾ red cabbage, core removed, finely shredded**
* **2 red onions, peeled and thinly sliced**
* **1tbsp sea salt**
* **2tbsp balsamic glaze**
* **2tbsp olive oil**
* **2tbsp each chopped parsley and dill**
* **1½tsp fennel seeds, toasted and lightly crushed**
* **250 g | 8.8 oz vacuum-packed beetroot in natural juice, cut into wedges**
* **1 cucumber, peeled, halved, deseeded and sliced**
* **150 g | 5.3 oz soft goats' cheese, sliced**
* **100 g | 3.5 oz pomegranate seeds**

1 Mix the red cabbage and onion in a large bowl, sprinkle over the sea salt and leave to soften for 15 mins. Rinse under cold water and squeeze dry with a clean tea towel or kitchen paper. Set aside.
2 Mix the balsamic, oil, herbs and fennel seeds together to create the dressing, season well and mix with the cabbage and onion. Set aside for 10 mins.
3 To serve, layer up the cabbage mixture with the beetroot and cucumber. Top with the goats' cheese and pomegranate seeds, and a good grinding of black pepper.
Per serving: Cals 229, Fat 10g, Sat fat 5g, Carbs 28g

TIP
You can use whatever pickle you have in the cupboard as long as it has small chunks in it

Giant sausage roll with cheese and pickle

A much-loved classic, this version benefits from the piquant tang of Branston inside!

Make 12 slices • Ready in 45 mins

* **375 g | 13 oz puff pastry**
* **FOR THE FILLING**
* **600 g | 22 oz pork sausage meat**
* **3tbsp Branston Small Chunk Pickle**
* **45 g | 1.5 oz Cheddar cheese, grated**
* **1 egg, beaten**

1 Heat the oven to 200°C/400°F/ Gas Mark 6. Roll out the pastry to a 30 x 22cm rectangle. Keep the trimmings for decoration. Chill the pastry while you make the filling.
2 Pat out half the sausage meat to 30cm in length on a piece of baking paper. This will make it easier to roll up.
3 Spoon the pickle over the centre of the sausage meat, then add a line of cheese through the centre. Pat over the rest of the sausage meat.
4 Use the baking paper to roll it into a long sausage shape, keeping the cheese and pickle in the middle as much as possible.
5 Brush the pastry edges with beaten egg then put the sausage meat in the centre and join the pastry around it.
6 Flip it over onto an oiled baking tray, brush with the egg, decorate with the pastry trimmings and glaze again.
7 Bake for 25-30 mins until golden brown and cooked all the way through. Allow to cool slightly before serving.
Per serving: Cals 458, Fat 25g, Sat fat 11g, Carbs 46g

Fig, leek and blue cheese tart

Ready-made pastry makes this festive dish so simple to prepare and it's sure to go down a storm.

Serves 8-10 • Ready in 1 hr 50 mins

✳ **500 g | 17 oz shortcrust pastry**
✳ **40 g | 1.4 oz butter**
✳ **2 leeks, finely sliced**
✳ **2tbsp sherry**
✳ **175 g | 6 oz ricotta cheese**
✳ **4 eggs, beaten**
✳ **100 ml | 3.5 fl oz double cream**
✳ **100 g | 3.5 oz blue cheese, crumbled (use a vegetarian cheese if serving veggies)**
✳ **1tsp chopped fresh thyme leaves**
✳ **3 figs, halved**

YOU WILL ALSO NEED
✳ **23cm loose-based tart tin, baking beans and baking parchment**

1 Heat the oven to 190°C/ 375°F/ Gas Mark 5. On a lightly floured surface, roll out the pastry to the thickness of a £1 coin. Transfer to the tin, then line with baking parchment, fill with baking beans and put on a baking tray. Bake blind for 20 mins.
2 Remove the beans and parchment, and bake for a further 10-15 mins until golden.
3 Reduce the oven temperature to 170°C/325°F/Gas Mark 3.

4 Meanwhile, melt the butter in a frying pan and gently cook the leeks for 10 mins until golden and caramelised. Add the sherry and cook for a further 2 mins to reduce, then remove from the heat.
5 Beat the ricotta, eggs and cream until smooth, then add the blue cheese, thyme and cooked leeks. Season and pour into the baked tart case.
6 Arrange the figs on top, brush each with a little oil and bake for 1 hr, or until the tart is set with a slight wobble. Remove the tart from the oven and allow to cool completely in the tin, before carefully turning out onto a platter to serve.
Per serving: Cals 525-420, Fat 39-30g, Sat fat 17-14g, Carbs 26-11g

TIP
If you don't have baking beans you can use rice instead

Smoked salmon terrine

Chunks of meaty hot smoked salmon add texture to this classic that never fails to impress.

Serves 8-10 • Ready in 30 mins, plus chilling

- ✳ **500 g | 17 oz smoked salmon**
- ✳ **300 g | 10.5 oz flaked hot smoked salmon**
- ✳ **300 g | 10.5 oz tub Philadelphia cream cheese**
- ✳ **2tbsp horseradish sauce**
- ✳ **zest and juice of 1 lemon**
- ✳ **small handful dill, leaves picked**
- ✳ **1½tsp pink peppercorns, crushed**
- ✳ **125 ml | 4.4 fl oz whipping cream**

YOU WILL ALSO NEED
- ✳ **28cm terrine dish or 900g loaf tin, double-lined with clingfilm**

1 In a food processor, blend 150 g of the smoked salmon and 150 g of the hot smoked salmon with the cream cheese, horseradish sauce, lemon zest, dill and peppercorns to make a smooth paste. Season with salt and pepper and add lemon juice, and transfer to a mixing bowl.
2 In another bowl, lightly whip the cream to soft peaks. Fold through the mixture and set aside.
3 Line the terrine dish with the remaining smoked salmon slices, allowing an overlap to fold over and almost cover the top.
4 Spoon half the salmon mixture into the terrine and spread to the edges. Place the remaining hot smoked salmon down the centre of the terrine in a neat line. Spoon the rest of the salmon mixture into the terrine, being careful not to disturb the hot smoked salmon. Smooth, then fold over the smoked salmon to cover the top. It doesn't matter if they don't meet. Wrap in the overhanging clingfilm and leave in the fridge overnight, weighed down with a board and some cans.
5 When ready to serve, turn out the terrine, remove the clingfilm and slice. Garnish with sliced chives.
Per serving: Cals 447, Fat 28g, Sat fat 9.1g, Carbs 31g

BOXING DAY
FEAST
FOR
friends

Wild rice salad with miso dressing

Kick off your meal in style with wild rice and an umami miso dressing.

Serves 4 • Ready in 45 mins

FOR THE DRESSING
* **2tbsp white miso paste**
* **2tbsp mild-flavoured honey**
* **4cm fresh ginger, peeled and finely grated**
* **2tbsp soy sauce**
* **Juice of 2 limes**

FOR THE SALAD
* **400 g | 14 oz pumpkin or squash, peeled and cut into 2cm cubes**
* **2 tbsp olive oil**
* **175 g | 6 oz wild rice**
* **100 g | 3.5 oz frozen edamame (soya) beans, defrosted**
* **1 head red chicory, trimmed and leaves separated**
* **4 spring onions, shredded**
* **1 avocado, stoned and diced**
* **2tbsp pumpkin seeds**

1 To make the dressing, simply whisk all the ingredients together and keep in the fridge until needed (it will keep in an airtight container for a week).
2 Heat the oven to 190°C/375°F/ Gas Mark 5. Toss the pumpkin or squash with the olive oil, season well and spread out on a baking sheet. Roast for about 30 mins until soft and turning brown. Set aside to cool.
3 Meanwhile, rinse the rice in a sieve, put in a pan and cover with 350ml water, add a good pinch of salt and bring to the boil. Cover, reduce the heat and simmer for about 30 mins, until the rice is plump and soft; add a little extra water if it appears to be drying out at any point.
4 Add the edamame beans to the rice and leave to cool. Gently fold the rice, beans and remaining ingredients together with the dressing and serve.
Per serving: Cals 400, Fat 16g, Sat Fat 3g, Carbs 48g

Veggie filo quiche

Using filo instead of shortcrust pastry means this quiche is super light.

Serves 6 • Ready in 40 mins

* ✳ **4 large sheets filo pastry**
* ✳ **25 g | 1 oz butter, melted**
* ✳ **125 g | 4.4 oz bag baby-leaf spinach**
* ✳ **6 eggs, whisked**
* ✳ **3 tbsp semi-skimmed milk**
* ✳ **Small bunch of mint, chopped**
* ✳ **100 g | 3.5 oz roasted artichoke hearts, halved**
* ✳ **100 g | 3.5 oz vegetarian feta, crumbled**
* ✳ **Salad leaves, to serve**

1 Heat the oven to 180˚C/350˚F/ Gas Mark 4. Line a loose-bottomed 24cm tart case with the filo sheets, leaving some overhang. Brush each layer of pastry with melted butter, then fold the overhang back into the case and brush with more butter.
2 Prick the spinach bag with a fork and microwave for 30 secs, until the leaves are just softened. Open the bag carefully and allow to cool slightly before handling.
3 Put the eggs, milk and mint into a large bowl, season with salt and freshly ground black pepper and whisk until combined. Arrange the spinach, artichoke hearts and feta in the filo case and pour over the egg mix. Cook in the oven for 20 mins. Serve the feta quiche hot or cold with a crisp green salad.
Per serving: Cals 241, Fat 15g, Sat Fat 6g, Carbs 14g

Roasted heritage carrots and parsnips with orange and za'atar

You can easily upgrade this to a veggie main dish by adding chickpeas and serving with couscous.

Serves 4 • Ready in 45 mins

- ✳ **500 g | 17 oz medium heritage carrots, cleaned and halved lengthways**
- ✳ **300 g | 10.5 oz parsnips, cleaned and halved lengthways**
- ✳ **1 orange, sliced**
- ✳ **2tsp cumin seeds**
- ✳ **1tbsp za'atar**
- ✳ **¼tsp crushed chillies**
- ✳ **4 garlic cloves**
- ✳ **Salt**
- ✳ **3tbsp olive oil**
- ✳ **1½tbsp honey**
- ✳ **5tbsp Greek yogurt**
- ✳ **1tbsp tahini**

1 Preheat the oven to 200°C/400°F/ Gas Mark 6. Put the carrots and parsnips in a roasting tin large enough to hold them in one layer.

2 Add the orange slices, cumin seeds, za'atar, chillies and garlic and season with salt, then toss thoroughly with the olive oil and honey. Roast for about 35-40 mins, until the vegetables are tender and golden.

3 Combine the yoghurt and tahini in a small bowl. Season lightly with salt and add a little crushed chilli, if you like. Serve alongside the roasted carrots and parsnips.

Per serving: Cals 264, Fat 13.5g, Sat Fat 3g, Carbs 28g

Apple and cinnamon crumbles

The perfect ending to any meal. If you're feeling extra indulgent, serve with a good quality vanilla ice cream.

Serves 4 · Ready in 55 mins

* 4 Bramley apples, peeled, cored, quartered and sliced
* 85 g | 3 oz golden caster sugar
* 2tbsp Calvados (apple brandy)
* 50 g | 1.7 oz stem ginger, finely chopped, plus 2tbsp ginger syrup from the jar
* 1tsp arrowroot mixed with 2tsp cold water

FOR THE BASE AND TOPPING
* 175 g | 6 oz plain flour
* 75 g | 2.6 oz chilled butter, cut into small chunks
* ½tsp ground cinnamon
* 1tbsp light muscovado sugar
* 50 g | 1.7 oz walnut halves, plus 4 halves, to decorate

YOU WILL NEED
* 4 x 10 cm metal rings and a buttered baking sheet

1 Heat the oven to 200°C/400°F/ Gas Mark 6. Put the apples, sugar and Calvados into a pan over a medium heat, cover and cook gently for 10-15 mins until the fruit is tender. Strain the apples in a sieve set over a bowl to catch the juices and leave to cool slightly.

2 To make the base and topping, put the flour and butter into a food processor and pulse to form crumbs. Add the cinnamon, sugar and walnuts and whizz to form coarse crumbs. Remove half the mixture from the food processor and set aside. Add the reserved ginger syrup to the crumble in the food processor and whizz to combine.

3 Press a quarter of this mixture into each metal ring to cover the base. add the stem ginger to the cooked apples and divide between each base. Sprinkle the reserved crumble mixture over the top. Bake for 15 mins, then top each one with a walnut half and bake for a few mins until the topping is pale golden.

4 Heat the reserved apple syrup with the arrowroot and stir continuously on a medium heat until thickened. Transfer each crumble to a plate, lift the ring of and spoon a little apple syrup over and around the crumbles before serving.
Per serving: Cals 627, Fat 25g, Sat Fat 11g, Carbs 95g